T0065781

OTHER BOOKS BY DENNIS KIMBRO

Think and Grow Rich: A Black Choice

Daily Motivations for African American Success

What Makes the Great Great

Dennis Kimbro

Harlem Moon
Broadway Books
NEW YORK

What Keeps Me Standing

*A Black
Grandmother's Guide
to Peace,
Hope & Inspiration*

PUBLISHED BY HARLEM MOON, an imprint of Broadway Books, a division of Random House, Inc.

A hardcover edition of this book was originally published in 2003 by Doubleday, a division of Random House, Inc. It is here reprinted by arrangement with Doubleday.

HARLEM MOON, BROADWAY BOOKS, and the HARLEM MOON logo, depicting a moon and a woman, are trademarks of Random House, Inc. The figure in the Harlem Moon logo is inspired by a graphic design by Aaron Douglas (1899–1979).

Visit our website at www.harlemmoon.com

First Harlem Moon trade paperback edition published 2005

Book design by Jennifer Ann Daddio

The Library of Congress has cataloged the hardcover as follows:
    What keeps me standing: a black grandmother's guide to peace, hope & inspiration / [compiled by] Dennis Kimbro.—1st ed.
        p.   cm.
    1. African Americans—Life skills guides. 2. Conduct of life.
3. Inspiration. 4. Peace of mind. 5. Hope. 6. African American women—Quotations. 7. African American women—Biography.
8. Grandmothers—United States—Quotations. 9. Grandmothers—United States—Biography. I. Kimbro, Dennis Paul, 1950–
E185.86.W43868 2003
170'.89'96073—dc21   2002041578

ISBN 0-7679-1238-1

To my late brother-in-law, Billy Joe. Thank God you never changed. Your prescription for living was so simple: Work hard and keep smiling. For more than two years we prayed and wondered what kept you standing. Now we know.

Acknowledgments

It's been written that a journey of a thousand miles begins with the first step. As I bring this project to a close, I've been blessed by a host of friends, family, and associates who made this journey with me. From day one, Jonathon Lazear and Christi Cardenas, my agents and my friends, saw to it that I put my best foot forward. Pauline Roberson not only spread the word, but saw to it that I didn't stumble out of the gate. My daughters Kelli, Ashanti, and Mackenzie have been there every step of the way. Their love and affection turned disappointment and stumbling blocks into stable and sound stepping-stones. For more than five years, David Smith continues to raise the bar and set the pace. Janet Hill, my editor, pushed the envelope and took a chance when others sidestepped the opportunity. While the competition wonders who moved the cheese, Janet has found it. To those grandmothers, nearly five hundred strong, who unselfishly shuffled tired feet and aching bones their entire lives so that we would be all the better for it. And finally, to Pat and Sarah, my two favorite grandmothers. My God, Kennedy is so lucky.

Contents

Chapter One:
Life Is the Greatest of All Statements

Chapter Two:
Live This Day

Chapter Three:
Hope

Chapter Four:
Count It All Joy!

Chapter Five:
Love Letter

Chapter Six:
Wanted: A Man

Chapter Seven:
Go and Do Likewise

Chapter Eight:
What Keeps Me Standing

Introduction

As if it happened yesterday, I can still remember the question that placed me upon my current path. It had been a busy time of year for each of us. The fall usually is. Although we could barely get together as a family, this mini-vacation had been on the books for weeks. As we left our North Carolina resort to head to our Atlanta home, my wife, Pat, flipped through an assortment of magazines while our two oldest daughters, Kelli and Kim, brought her up-to-date on the latest college fashions. MacKenzie, our ninth grader and our youngest, was immersed in a *USA Today*, trying to make sense of the latest presidential polls. As for me, my mind was fixated upon upcoming speaking engagements and book signings. I had averaged at least two presentations a week for God knows how long, and I felt blessed to be able to take a few days off. Looking up from her newspaper, MacKenzie asked, "Dad, who are you going to vote for—President Clinton or Bob Dole?"

Caught off guard, I returned her question. "I don't know, Mac. Who should I vote for?"

"Well, if I could vote, I know exactly how I would cast my ballot. I would elect Grandma Mary president, and Grandma Ruby vice president." Amused by her thinking, I asked why.

"Because they know everything," she explained. "Grandma Mary helps me with my homework, and Grandma Ruby makes me feel special." I pinched my daughter's cheek, tossed her words over in my mind, and continued the four-hour drive. The following morning as I prepared to catch yet another flight to another city, I grabbed pad and pen, and wrote a few words. Through the eyes of a child I was given the scope of my fourth book.

As reflected in earlier works, I've always been attracted to the subjects of success and achievement. I have interviewed peak performers in a variety of fields seeking to pinpoint the cause of their success. Now my effort takes on new meaning. For the past five years, I've shifted my focus from those highly touted entrepreneurs, corporate climbers, and peak performers whom I have examined in the past, to target those individuals who truly epitomize the human spirit: one thousand black grandmothers!

In all honesty, I did not write this book. I wish I had. Had I written this book I would be quite proud. Too proud for anyone to imagine. No, this is the work of hands far more skilled than my own; souls too deep, insights too worldly for me to comprehend. My part was minimal, at best. I didn't bring anything special to the table. I was an innocent bystander seated in the corner taking notes—a silent listener. A role that I do not consider a task but an honor, an undeserved privilege. I've been allowed to sit at the council of elders and drink from their endless fountain of wisdom.

No matter how I tried to speak in my own voice, I found it difficult and sometimes useless to edit a text and offer words that simply could not be improved upon. Furthermore, I now realize that my previous writings were neither original nor unique. *How could they be?* Someone else had been there before with better ideas that could only be revived, recycled, or renewed. I am not discouraged. I know my place. No ego here. My sole purpose was to galvanize this collection of rich ideas into a simple, seamless volume and offer it to you, the reader—God's child—as a good and perfect gift. Frankly, I am shocked that no one had yet written a book such as this. What strikes me is that the ideals formulated by this generation gone by remain contemporary in every sense. Their words and beliefs are completely untarnished by the passage of time. Clearly, here lies the last self-help book the world will ever need.

No, I did not and *could not* pen such a text. But one thousand women could—and did! *Black women*. Each skilled in the art of living. Everyday folks who got up early, stayed up late, and who did a whole lot in between. On average, each is a grandmother several times over, and at least sixty years of age. Each a spiritual sage with a plumb moral compass who sought neither fame nor fortune.

Each black grandmother was given the same request: If you had to write a letter to your children or to the next generation, what would you say? What would you tell them? Would you offer the same words of advice given to you during your youth? Or, how about a few helpful hints that lifted your spirits during those tougher moments? Or, would you share your own personal philosophy for living? Straightforward or humorous, prose or poetry, simple or profound, what would you say if you could write a *single letter to your children or your children's children* about continuity and caring, life and living?

Would you tell your sons and daughters to count their blessings so that they may not only appreciate what has been given to them but, in turn, they may want to do something for those less fortunate? Would you tell your children that every human being is a miracle of creation, a marvel to behold, a priceless treasure, created for a purpose? Would you tell them that they are capable of great wonders; that they can *be* anything, *do* anything, *have* anything they wish—provided they are willing to pay the price for its attainment? Would you tell them that each of us is charged with the duty of leaving this world a little bit better than we found it? Would you tell them to use their greatest power wisely—*the power of choice?* With this power each of us has been placed slightly below the angels, blessed with the divine gift of choosing our own destiny.

Would you tell them that it's okay to believe in Santa Claus, the tooth fairy, as well as each other, and that dreams do come true? And, as they chase their dreams, would you tell them to never, never give up or to lose faith or surrender the desires of their heart? Moreover, would you tell them to humble themselves before their God and pray, not only for the desires of their heart, but for understanding and guidance?

Would you tell them to enjoy this day, for this is the day the Lord has made? Would you tell them to fulfill life's greatest task: the need to love and to be loved? If you could write one letter, one note, one word of advice, one bit of instruction for living, what would you say?

Countless black grandmothers carved out a piece of their day in order to address these simple questions. These contributors gave of themselves to their children, and to all of us. Their message tells a story of peace, hope, understanding, and how to navigate the rough patches of life. They instruct how to do well by doing good. These messages come from a diverse group of black women—some were cooks, some were domestics, and more than a few had and continue to labor on an assembly line, many times the third shift. A handful were financially independent, but the majority were only a day's march ahead of hard times. There were doctors and lawyers, teachers and nurses. I received letters from elderly women who not only wrote of their sons and grandsons in prison, but who had served time themselves. On another score, I felt privileged to take in the thoughts of a black woman who served as a delegate to the 2000 Republican National Convention. Even in her autumn years she spoke of the impact that *her* grandmother had on her life. I even received a letter from the vice-mayor of Deltona, Florida, Lucille Wheatley, who had won the post in her midsixties. Like her peers, she spoke of faith and spirituality. Another who shared her thoughts is the Mayor of Orange, Texas, Essie Bellfield. When it comes to living, she, like her sisters, can see quite clearly. Their hearts have 20-20 vision.

Within these pages you will find the words of a seventy-five-year *young* Chicago-based grandmother who walks ten crisp miles a day. Not to be outdone by one Lucille Singleton, a retired domestic who, regardless of rain or shine, steps out of her Manhattan apartment at 4 a.m. sharp, "to squeeze in her three-mile workout." An inspiration to everyone in her neighborhood, Miss Singleton didn't take up running until age seventy. Six years later, at the prodding of the New York Road Runners club, where she volunteers her time and when many half her age find it difficult to run around the block, she completed the famed New York City Marathon in a respectable eight hours and two minutes.

In the fifth chapter your heart will be moved by two grandmothers, kindred spirits, who felt the universal calling to this project. Their letters are a testimony that love knows no color.

Letters arrived not only from America, but from Canada, the Caribbean, and even West Africa. The majority of letters were sent by mail. Some were faxed, several were hand delivered, and a few, surprisingly, were e-mailed. One letter was stamped CERTIFIED SPECIAL DELIVERY. Four women from a Brooklyn, New York, housing project, sat around a kitchen table and recorded their thoughts on audio cassette, and sent me the cassette in place of their letters. Grandmothers wrote their letters on personalized stationery as well as scrap paper and greeting cards. I also received letters written by hands that were gnarled and disfigured by arthritis and conceived by minds numbed by Alzheimer's disease. Responses were offered by grandmothers who are well and by those who were, and remain, quite ill. Five grandmothers, may they rest in peace, shared their last dying words.

Most letters were handwritten, some were typed, and a handful were barely legible. One tender response was sent by an eighty-year-old great-great-grandmother composed on her personal computer. More than a few letters were crafted at church. Some were drafted at senior citizens' facilities and nursing homes, while the majority were written at day's end seated on the edge of a bed. Here, God was obviously at work. Many grandmothers had so much on their minds, that they called me direct. The words and thoughts of a unique group of thinkers are here. Whether educated or not, each viewed education as the ticket up and out. Some of the wisest words and most compelling lessons I read did not come from Ivy League grads or highly trained minds. On the contrary, my instructions came from poor black women sixty years and older, educated in the school of life. Valedictorians all, in the academy of hard knocks. Their teacher was struggle, their books were hope, and their pencils were sharpened by prayer. These truth seekers teach us once again, at a time when we need reminding, the importance of kindness and perseverance, of honesty and hope, of respect and integrity, of right and wrong.

They spoke of their roots in similar rural towns and shared the events that shaped their lives. They quoted their parents, grandparents, as well as their pastor. They paraphrased Maya Angelou, Benjamin Mays, Marian Wright Edelman, Martin Luther King, Jr., Iyanla Vanzant, T. D. Jakes, and their God. They provided prayers, poems, and Scripture; but most important, they shared a similar prescription for living that will open the doors to hope, peace, and contentment and give us the ability to fulfill our dreams.

One might wonder, what is to be gained by utilizing the wisdom passed down by others? Why not continue to live day by day, taking things as they come? The answer is manifold and the lesson is plain: Those best suited to direct, lead, and nurture others are not those who may have studied life in a book. On the contrary, the best guides are those individuals who have lived life and who possess the stripes to prove it. The shortest path to becoming somebody is to know whom to follow. Our stay on this planet is far too brief, and the time given to us, all too short. Life demands that we thirst for knowledge. I remember reading somewhere that a single conversation with the insightful is worth a year's study of books. Ultimately, we owe the most to those who make us become what we can become; who, regardless of the situation or circumstances, never lower expectations. Whatever little knowledge we have acquired is due to the knowledge, thoughts, and ideas written by those gone before us.

Today as we face life's innumerable challenges, when so many of us are troubled, uncertain, and confused, the rich deposits of inspiration offered by preceding generations take on a new and vital importance. In a world awash with insecurity and in search of acceptance, and a society where people are often judged by what they own and who they know, there has never been a time when the tried and true philosophies of the past were more urgently needed to supply perspective and understanding. *What Keeps*

Me Standing is a concise and easy-to-understand guide to life's most probing question: *How then, shall we live?* The door to a fulfilling life lies before you, and the thoughts from these gentle souls will supply the eternal key.

Louder than words, *What Keeps Me Standing* is not a book to be consumed in one or two sittings. Nor does it suggest turning back the clock or rejecting the progress and benefits of a modern era. Rather, it is a supplement to keep at your bedside, a treasure trove to dip into as needed. It is a timeless story that transcends religious, national, and ethnic boundaries. Here is a book that will be both feared and welcomed. Feared because the reader will realize the legacy to which it is tied and the standards he feels responsible to uphold. But welcomed because its central message encourages each of us to honor and emulate our forebears. We can do no better than to pass along what has been given to us: a positive framework for living. Open this text to any page and savor its richness, digest its tender phrases. Here is a book meant to be read, absorbed, and then mulled over until all is right within your soul. And whether you agree with this message or not, as you turn each page, please be willing to consider a new outlook. Some may understand what this wise sage says, but a true student will understand what she feels. Transformation is a slow process. Take as long as you need but do be gentle with yourself. Allow your heart, mind, and spirit to process each lesson before returning for more.

If books bore you, this book won't. If few books move you, this book will. If words don't change your life, these will drive you on. So often we find ourselves in a world in which we feel inadequate, powerless, unloved, and lost. Could this be your destiny? Do you wander in emptiness, occasionally bumping into another weary traveler on your narrow road who is even more desperate than you? If you have felt weak, abandoned, and unloved, then take heart. Within these pages lie traceable tracks that will help the most vanquished soul navigate life's most challenging passages.

Have you lost your way? *What Keeps Me Standing* will guide your feet. Have your lost your faith? Then read on. In due time your faith will be renewed. Are you confused? Take heart. You hold in your hands a message from the past for a new millennium, a rich merger of heartfelt love and compassion that allows you to seek the deeper meaning behind life's dilemmas. These inscriptions will permit you to meet the challenges of the day and work out your own salvation. Does despair cling at your heels? Here lies your good fortune. Meditate on the counsel contained within and you will find spiritual abundance, a storehouse of fortitude, and a floodlight that brightens the path to empowerment. So settle down for a remarkable journey through centuries of wisdom. Allow your imagination to carry you beyond words on a page. Listen to the music of the writers' voices—feel the delivery, the inflection, the pitch, the cadence, the changing rhythm, the pulse, and, most of all, the passion that stirred the heart of a race and continues to leave an indelible mark.

These black grandmothers understand life so well. Irresistibly lovable, you can't touch them without touching their spirit. Their solution to any problem can be found somewhere between the Bible, education, and hard work—the three most important legs on their stools. No nonsense, no foolishness, no false airs, and no fluff. Just principles. "I can be me better than anyone else," one grandmother writes, "so there is no need to impress anyone." You get the picture. Always substance over style. When it comes to pain they don't even bother to wince. For them, hard times come easy, and they are still standing even in the worst of times. It is from this wealth of experience that I have siphoned off words of wisdom. Hopefully, they will empower others to run on fractured legs, crawl on bruised knees, and stand on swollen feet.

September 5, 1998
Birmingham, AL

WHY I WAS PLACED ON EARTH.
SURVIVING IS EASY; LIVING IS DIFFICULT.

I've always felt that the best letters are those that may have never been written. With that in mind, my words may not make a difference to you but the Lord placed these thoughts in my heart to at least try. I've tried to live my life as an example to others. I tried to be a devoted wife, loving and thoughtful. I've tried to be a good mother, striving to raise caring, kind, and considerate children. I've tried to be a good person, though many times I've stumbled. Most of all, I've tried to be a witness; to play my part; to live purely, humbly, and without regret. Our lives are our witness, and our witness is our legacy. It is what lives on in the world after we have departed.

There was a time in my life when I searched for direction. As a faith-filled twenty-year-old, I had set my sights on becoming a nurse. But as a black woman with an eleventh-grade education, there would be no American dream for me. Not in the 1950's, and definitely not in Birmingham, Alabama. That would be too much to ask. Back then, Birmingham's heart was as hard as steel. It was a tough place for black folks to live. Not only was the city racially divided, it was the home to the largest Ku Klux Klan chapter in the nation. Consequently, the only job I could find would be to sweep and mop the floors of the city's mental health hospital. There I stayed for God knows how long, sweeping, dusting, and carrying out my duties to the best of my ability, always hoping for brighter days. But what I didn't count on when I took the job was that it would also become my ministry—the kindling and spark needed to ignite a soul.

During my stay, a wealthy white physician had been admitted to the facility. After thirty years of marriage his wife had an affair which led to his nervous breakdown. I felt so sorry for him. The story was in all the

papers. His doctors tried all types of treatments and medication but with
little success. He had completely withdrawn. Every day, when I made my
rounds with my mop and bucket, I would visit with him. "Snap out of
it," I would tell him. "You don't belong here. You've got so much to live
for. You need to pick up the pieces and get on with your life." I guess he
stayed there for nearly five years until one day, he slowly began to open
up. A short time later his doctors discharged him. They said he had made
a complete and full recovery. As he gathered his belongings and said his
good-byes he waited until everyone had turned their head. Then, without
any warning, he walked over to me and placed a one hundred dollar bill
into my hand.

"What are you doing?" I asked.

"That's my way of saying thank you," he whispered. "If it weren't for
you there's no way I would be leaving. You did more for me than any of
these so-called trained professionals." And, with that, he hugged me and
left.

Surviving is easy; living can be difficult. We are so conditioned to
think that our lives revolve around great moments. But great moments often catch us off guard. Just think: When that wealthy white doctor embraced me, a poor black woman in that southern hospital nearly fifty
years ago, it was possible to believe that I had been placed on earth for
the sole purpose of helping him regain his sanity. I may never do anything in my life that is more important.

You never know the power you possess to heal a human heart. Regardless where life may lead, you've got a role to play. Sometimes circumstances won't allow you to reach back, but they should never stop you
from reaching over.

You are a child of God, and you do matter . . .
Minnie Player

October 1, 1998
Baltimore, MD

LIFE IS THE GREATEST OF ALL
STATEMENTS; MAKE SURE YOURS
SPEAKS VOLUMES.

You've known me, faults and all, for the better part of thirty years. More than anyone else, you know there are many questions regarding life that I alone cannot answer. I'm the first to admit, I'm not extraordinarily gifted in any single area. It's true, I did graduate from college during a time when so few dared to look beyond high school. For that accomplishment I am most grateful and proud. But each time I gaze at my diploma, I realize that I am still a student, still learning every day how to be human. And yes, I am equally proud to proclaim that your grandfather and I have been united in wedded bliss for fifty-four years. I've tried my best to live out my marriage vows. I've tried to be more than a good wife, seeking also to be my mate's best friend.

In spite of my seventy years and these accomplishments, I suppose the only subject I can discuss with any amount of certainty would be living itself. So here's the bottom line: Get a life!

Not just any life, but a good life. A blessed life. A life built with laughter and warmth. Two powerful qualities. You're the only person on earth capable of living it. Life is glorious and no one has any business taking it for granted.

Get a life. A life that keeps the faith and prays daily. A life that asks not for material possessions but for guidance, knowledge, and wisdom. A life overflowing with self-control, self-respect, and confidence. Trust me on this one. You can do all things.

Get a life. A life not based upon money, but on how much you can give. A life filled with compassion and generosity, which you can share freely. A life that is synonymous with justice. One that will lead marches and right the wrongs of everyday people. All of us want to do well. But if we do not do good, then doing well will never be enough. Get a life that lives by my grandfather's words: "If you've got a lazy bone in your body, cut it out." It's so easy to waste our time, our days, our hours, and minutes. Take my word for it: the clock is ticking. Waste not another moment. It's a mistake to depend on others, so hold up your end of the bargain and get to work no matter how tedious the task.

Get a life. A life that is fearless; one that will not be burdened by risk or failure, no matter how huge, regardless of how many. A life that will never condemn; one that can ask for forgiveness and grant it just the same. A life that knows the value of silence in the face of others' missteps. One that is capable of passing life's toughest test: patience. It's a simple virtue that I practice every day, praying that you will begin to pull your life together and overcome your addiction.

If you are to benefit from this journey, get a life that lives by every word of His commandments; a life that demonstrates grace and mercy. One that can walk in the company of greatness yet is humble enough to be measured by the true Son—He that is first and last; last and first. This is the standard by which you and I will be judged. So there you have it. Words from someone who may not have done much or earned much but has experienced plenty. If you will take heart and be guided by all that you have read, you will not be disappointed.

Life is the greatest of all statements. Make sure yours speaks volumes,

Marian Scarborough

Chapter One

Life
Is the
Greatest
of All
Statements

ow late we grow smart. To be honest, there were times when I thought I knew everything. However, after absorbing the letters contained within this passage, I found I knew nothing. And I am not alone. Millions of people blessed with the miracle of sight never really see the world. Millions with the innate capacity to love, and to know the joy that love brings, wait too long to express it. Too frequently, a visit to a nursing home will reveal the following: Patients who realize that their days are drawing to a close will often say, "I waited too long to start living." You should find their remarks strange. What they're really saying is that they failed to enjoy life even during those years that they were living it most fully. It's like the person who puts the best china and silverware away for some rare, special occasion. Unfortunately, these individuals die before it is ever used.

Few people, it seems, develop an awareness for living. While possessing the greatest gift—life itself—they pass through their days like robots. Even worse, their actions clearly demonstrate that they don't have the slightest idea of life's value, let alone an awareness that life is to be treasured and enjoyed each and every day. It's only when their days grow short and their hour draws near that life's precious value begins to take hold. I find it amazing, but most of us place the greatest value on the cheapest commodities—possessions, that if lost or stolen could easily be replaced—while the greatest gift of all goes unnoticed. The most fortunate people in the world are those who have been taught to place value where it belongs—on an awareness for living.

So if you are about to graduate from high school or college, consider these letters the homework assignment you failed to complete and the commencement speech you never heard. If you've grown weary of an uninspiring religion and find your spirit thirsting for re-

newal, here's the sermon you missed. If your parents failed to provide the loving guidance and sense of direction that is necessary for fulfillment in today's embattled world, here is the firm but tender heart-to-heart talk you should have received in your youth. At last your life and your future are in your hands—and yours alone. You now possess the power and the means to make all your tomorrows a special heaven on earth. You may now walk with head high and shoulders erect toward the future you deserve. Live your life well!

❖   ❖   ❖

October 16, 1998
Glenmora, LA

WHAT I LEARNED ABOUT LIFE AND SUCCESS IN THE COTTON FIELDS OF LOUISIANA

Mother used to say, "You will hear me long after I am gone." The first time I heard these words I had no idea what she meant. When conveying the facts of life, my mother always spoke in parables and proverbs. This remarkable statement would be an important lesson that neither of us would verbalize during her lifetime. Now, fifty years have come and gone, and I realize she could not have taught me in a more excellent way. As I look back from my lofty perch in academia, sitting behind a mahogany desk in a high-back leather chair, surrounded by walls draped with citations, mementos, and diplomas, my hearing is as sharp as ever. I can only admire the wisdom and subtlety my mother displayed as she prepared me for the future. "You may not agree with all I've got to say, but sooner or later my words will ring true," was the message my mother was trying to convey.

In those days, I was as full of questions as my mother was of answers. A lesser individual would've knuckled under due to the stress and strain long ago, and certainly wouldn't have had the time to guide me. A pillar of strength, here stood a woman who could've easily been overwhelmed with the responsibilities of earning a living, caring for her children, and just plain keeping her head above water. Whoever said no one is irreplaceable never met my mother. Though she is no longer with me, her advice continues to make a difference in unexpected and unexplained ways.

Like those before me, I began picking cotton as a young girl growing up in Louisiana. I was barely twelve years old. Throughout my childhood, though money and means were rare commodities, hard work could be found in abundance. Now, I don't know if you've ever toiled in the cotton fields but Lord, have mercy, I can think of a thousand jobs—from washing clothes to cooking and cleaning, to sweating away in the cabbage patch, you name it—I'd rather do. I've lived and worked the world over and, if I never pick an ounce of cotton in my life again, that would be fine with me. Somehow my mother sensed my disdain. "There's more to picking cotton," she would say, "than just filling a sack. If you look hard and long enough you will find a lesson or two." There was little chance that I would live out my life in those hot and humid cotton fields of central Louisiana, but once again I would lean on my mother's words to pull me through.

The human journey is short. We no sooner realize that we are here than it is time for us to go. Though you may never lift a cotton sack in your life, I pray that you will appreciate and benefit from the pearls of wisdom I plucked from the cotton fields of Louisiana:

> LESSON ONE: The workday began at 3 a.m. sharp, and concluded somewhere between 5 and 6 p.m. The foreman's truck that carried me and other workers to the fields came bright and early and expected each worker to be on time. At an early age I was taught the value of discipline: If I failed to show up at the appointed hour that workday would be rendered wasted. I soon discovered "on time" means on time and success in any endeavor begins early and stays late.

LESSON TWO: Never expect something for nothing. At the conclusion of each workday, within full view of everyone, each sack of cotton was weighed. One large sack—a good day's effort—brought at least three dollars, money I desperately needed. But each sack had to be filled with clean, dry cotton. Though human nature might tempt one to cut corners (I've seen field hands throw rocks and dirt into their sacks in an effort to add to their total weight), eventually their shortcuts and deception were uncovered. Never look for or expect more than what you put in. Never expect easy money, success without working, or to get rich quick.

LESSON THREE: I was raised in a rundown clapboard house. As I lay in bed each night I could see the evening stars through my roof and the chickens beneath the floor. I dared not complain. Mother was doing the best she could. The following morning, as I moved from row to row with that bag of cotton on my shoulders, I carried my dreams for a better world with me. I took an inward journey and unleashed the power of my mind. I pictured a home in an upscale neighborhood. A house complete with indoor plumbing, carpeted floors, freshly painted walls, topped off with a huge kitchen featuring the latest appliances. As my imagination ran wild I came to rely on a spiritual secret: Trust the unseen more than the visible. I may have never openly shared my dreams, but I knew this was the life I was meant to live. Now, in more ways than one, I finally feel at home. Today, I live in the house that I envisioned—complete with all the bells and whistles—down to the smallest detail. And to think I began laying the foundation nearly half a century ago. It is never too late to become the person you were meant to be. Let your imagination soar. It is the secret language of the soul.

LESSON FOUR: Truth be known, I wasn't the fastest cotton picker in the field. To be honest, not only was I the slowest, but my inability to develop a rhythm (yes, there is a rhythm to picking cotton) many times caused bottlenecks as I struggled from row to endless row. To my surprise the older workers didn't seem to mind. As a matter of fact, they overlooked my shortcomings and wrapped me in a blanket of encouragement. Collectively, they knew of my dreams of going to college, and eventually earning a graduate degree. To them, I represented faith and hope for the future. Not just my future, but the future for every overworked and underpaid brother and sister who slaved away in those fields. With my head down, and back and knees aching, I can still hear them leading me on: "Come on, Baby. You can do it! You're gonna make it." Their words of hope and redemption touched me in a healing way. Since the day I set foot on the Grambling State University campus to the day I walked across the stage at Texas Southern University to receive my doctorate degree, I have lived by this lesson. Like those field hands who had the utmost faith in me, their daily words of encouragement set the tone for all that I would accomplish. On a word and a prayer, I pressed on.

Well, my mother was right. "There's more to picking cotton than just filling a sack." It was my mother who not only pointed me to the cotton fields but who knew I would uncover a number of life-changing lessons as well. Within each of us blooms a wellspring of abundance and opportunity. For in each of us rests a deeply personal dream waiting to be plucked. When we cherish our dreams and invest in hard work, faith, and discipline, we will achieve long-lasting success.

I have faith that you will hear my words long after I am gone,
Doris Price, Ph.D.

September 10, 1998
Nashville, TN

TO DARE GUIDE A LIFE

Well, where do I start? The best advice I've been given rests on the following: Life is oh so precious. In that brief space of time between birth and death each of us discovers life's true meaning. My life has been enriched by the lives I've touched, shaped, and molded in more than forty years of teaching. It has been gratifying to see those whom I have taught discover their unique talents and gifts. My job was no less than that of my parents who had the daunting task of convincing me, though I couldn't eat at certain lunch counters or use public restrooms or participate in a system that overlooked my abilities that, in spite of it all the indignities and injustice, somehow, someway, I could still reach my goals. No small chore.

Only a few, if any, of the lives that I've embraced will approximate the discoveries of a George Washington Carver or the commitment and contributions of a Dr. King, a Booker T. Washington or a Harriet Tubman. Nonetheless, driven by a compulsion for success, many of my former students have blossomed into doctors, lawyers, corporate executives, and public servants. To dare guide a life and to help a young child discover his or her innate gifts is especially meaningful to me. This is the best way to put meaning into your life. The Man Above only asks that we begin.

Cora R. Goodwin

April 25, 2001
Baltimore, MD

A GOOD BOOK IS YOUR MOST TREASURED POSSESSION

The year was 1933—the bottom of the Great Depression. My father, born and raised in Barbados, came to this country with high hopes and even higher expectations. Though his entrepreneurial dreams fell short, my father was determined that his journey to America would not be in vain. After all, here was a man who had immigrated to the U.S. from Barbados at the turn of the century and immediately experienced a string of business failures. Here was a man who didn't think twice when faced with the prospects of risking his life to go abroad in order to feed his family. Before immigrating to the U.S., he took a job nearly one thousand miles away to work on the Panama Canal. Like thousands of ditch diggers who fought the jungle heat, disease-carrying mosquitoes, and the constant threat of landslides, he dug day and night until his blistered hands were nearly covered with blood. It's amazing what you'll do when responsibilities must be met. Years later he moved his family to Harlem and set his sights on the ministry. After my grandmother died from an insidious tuberculosis outbreak, my mother, a stately-looking woman from Jamaica, came to the U.S. with her God-mother through Ellis Island. Dedicated to educating her children, she took a job as a Gregg Shorthand stenographer for a small New York City law firm. Her earnings were meager but they enabled our survival.

Together, my parents had many endearing qualities—hardworking, thrift, loyalty to each other, and high moral standards—not to mention their love of learning and books. My father ruled his roost with both an iron fist and a velvet glove. He was hell-bent on personal achievement. He had a thick, old leather strap that he judiciously applied whenever we willfully broke the rules. My brothers, sisters, and I were considered to be well

mannered and, on numerous occasions, our parents were complimented as
to our impeccable deportment. My fondest memories of my mother were
our trips to the library where she made sure that her children had collected
their share of positive reading material. I can still remember her reading to
us from an old, dusty red book brought from her native land which pro-
filed African kings and queens. If time permitted, she would shuffle us off
to the Museum of Natural History where our little inquisitive minds
would run wild. We were also regulars at the Schomburg Library on 135th
Street and Lenox, and even took picnics at Grant's Tomb overlooking the
Hudson. On Sunday afternoons after church, in Carnegie Hall, our entire
family could usually be found in the front row listening to the classical
music of Chopin or Grieg, or pondering the words of great orators or inspiring poets of the day who happened to be in the area, leaving an even
bigger imprint on our lives. This was the era of the Harlem Renaissance
during which intellectual giants like Countee Cullen, Langston Hughes,
and Paul Lawrence Dunbar filled many auditoriums and churches. Few can
remember that in 1951 W. E. B. Du Bois, the famed educator and activist,
ran for the New York Senate seat as a third-party candidate. Father insisted that I work on Dr. Du Bois' campaign.

Among family and friends my father's reading habits were legendary.
All the great black classics could be found on our dining room table. In-
tellectually, he was hard to impress and heaven forbid if you ever used
poor grammar or gave less than your best. My father would stop dead in
his tracks. Some find it hard to believe, but he routinely held weekly
spelling bees among his nine children. Once, he insisted that we master a
word twenty-three letters long. And our reward? Just more hugs, praise,
and even higher expectations. A good book, he felt, is your most treasured possession. To him, nothing was worse than a lazy mind.

When it came to continuous learning my parents couldn't have written a better script. Their personal attention, grounded in history and culture, not only inflated our tiny egos, but inspired us to go higher. By the
time I had completed elementary school I had been skipped twice! And,

thanks to their steady hand, I have studied at Oxford, England, and next year—at the ripe age of eighty—I expect to complete my master's degree in education from the University of Maryland.

Like my parents, I've always been quite fond of reading and the power of one book to make a difference. Reading allows me to reconnect and step back and gain perspective. But choosing a favorite book is an impossibility. Simply put, there's no easy way to take a lifetime of reading and single out a handful of great books as the most influential in my life. However, I've managed to select a few, those works that had a profound effect on me and that I believe will be equally meaningful to you . . .

1. *Mis-Education of the Negro* by Carter G. Woodson. I love when you pick up a book and, by the end of the first page, you're firmly planted in the world of the writer. Written nearly a half-century ago, the author raises questions that we are trying to answer today. Woodson's astonishing truth literally changed my mind about everything under the sun. If you ever wanted to know the impact of slavery on the Black American psyche this book would be a good place to start. Far ahead of its time, this is a must read.

2. *The Souls of Black Folk* by W. E. B. Du Bois. One of the most prophetic and influential works in American literature. Written at the turn of the century, Du Bois dares as no one has dared before to describe the magnitude of racism on every level of society, and demands an end to it. Every word is a call to arms and a cry of the heart.

3. *The Mother of Us All: A History of Queen Nanny* by Karla Gottlieb. Talk about inspiring, I can't get over the amount of courage exhibited by a single soul with freedom on her mind. An expose of slavery in the Carribean, this remarkable book profiles an African woman who stood up against the British and led the Maroons to freedom. This may be a stretch, but if it weren't for women like Queen Nanny who pushed forward in a time when all people of

color were kept in their place, I wouldn't be where I am today. Liberating and encouraging, I couldn't put it down.

4. The writings of J. A. Rogers and John Henry Clarke. I don't care if you lived through the civil rights movement or not, any book by these true African-American scholars is yet another reason to be proud.

So, to my seven children (Tylers and Alloteys), twenty-three grandchildren and four great-grandchildren, as you embark on the new millennium never has there been greater need for knowledge and understanding. When you plunge into a good book, let yourself go. You will be surprised where your mind takes you. Perhaps now would be a good time to ask, What book are you reading?

Enid M. Tyler

❧   ❧   ❧

March 18, 2000
Houston, TX

LOOK WHERE YOU CAME FROM

I fully realize that the odds are exceedingly high you will never read my words or the contents of this letter and yet, although I have so very little of anything, I still have hope. If my letter lies unopened on your nightstand when I depart from this world, then it will be up to the good Lord to determine whether or not your eyes and heart will benefit from my efforts. I can only pray.

At last your life and your future are in your hands—and yours alone. You now possess the power and the means to make all your tomorrows a special heaven on earth. You may now walk with head high and shoulders erect toward the future you deserve. Live your life well!

Most people don't go through life—they just go through an existence.
The following passage was taken from my favorite book, *Daughters of the
Dust*, by Julie Dash [New York: Penguin/Putnam, 1999]. It has been the
foundation of my life, and now, I offer it to you:

*If you've ever doubted your ability to survive, look where you came from. Don't
limit yourself to parents and grandparents, go all the way back to your roots. In
your family line is the genius of those who were born into a barren land and built
the pyramids. In the oasis of your mind is the consciousness of those who charted the
stars, kept time by the sun and the moon. In the center of your being is the strength
of those who planted crops, tilled the fields, and banqueted on what others discarded.
In the light of your heart is the love of those who bore the children who were sold
away only to one day hang from a tree. In the cells of your bloodstream is the memory of those who weathered the voyage, stood on the blocks, found their way through
the forest, and took their case to the Supreme Court. With what you've got going for
you, what in the world are you worrying about?*

> You move in the power of a mighty past,
> Bessie Adam Burks

❖   ❖   ❖

October 10, 2000
Legon-Accra
Ghana, West Africa

HWE WO HO SO YIYE

My name is Adelaide Afua Gyaunea. I am better known as Adelaide
Maute after I adopted my late husband's name. I was born in Ghana, West
Africa. I am ninety-five years old. Though my journey has been anything
but easy, I've got few complaints. I would like to believe that I fought the

good fight and that I've held my own. The years have made me sensitive to the tender touch of the human spirit because I decided long ago to live—or at least try to live—with dignity, respect, courage, and composure. I've been blessed with four children, eleven grandchildren, and so many great-grandchildren that I can hardly keep up with them. But if I could have a moment with each, I would try to offer the missing piece to life's puzzle: "Hwe Wo Ho So Yiye," which means: You are special.

Never place limits on yourself or run from failure. We envy the men and women who have achieved success, but we fail to see the heartaches and disappointments buried beneath their triumph. Anyone can, given an opportunity and the proper motivation, achieve some measure of success and happiness. Life is what you make it. Don't bother to worry; it is a waste of time. The longer you carry a problem, the heavier it gets. Be careful, and maintain a reasonable sense of health and goodwill. And finally, if you pursue happiness and success, they will forever elude you. But if you focus on your family, the needs of others, and doing the very best you can, happiness and success will beat a path to your door. God has a special plan for you. Believe me, I know.

I must go now. My eyesight is poor and my hand is beginning to tremble. I hope you will consider my words. You won't be disappointed.

A. G. Maute

❖   ❖   ❖

December 6, 1998
Hampton, VA

THIS LETTER IS A GIFT OF HAPPINESS

Hopefully, you will view my letter as a gift, a gift unlike any you will ever receive. This letter is a gift of happiness. To be honest, I cannot offer you happiness, no one can. That, you must find for yourself. But what I can do is share the manner in which happiness may be provided as you journey through life. I did not find these keys alone, they were passed down from generations gone long before. Your ancestors left you and me a legacy, not in material possessions or family treasures, but through a message of inspiration. These words have sustained me and, Lord willing, will carry you through each and every day of your life:

1. Be thankful. Never complain or despair about what you may lack. Sometimes not getting what you want can be a stroke of luck. Instead thank God for what you've been given. Give thanks every day for the Creator's constant stream of blessings. Never underestimate the power of the gifts that abide within. Pray for what you need but always pray to stay in the center of God's will.

2. Be responsible. Take care of what you've been given. If you open it, close it; if you break it, admit it and fix it. If you make a mess, clean it up. If you borrow it, return it.

3. Be friendly and helpful to others regardless of their station in life. Remember, the Lord created each of us, therefore never belittle anyone. Look for the best in all mankind.

4. Strive for the best. You may falter or stumble along the way. If so, pick yourself up and start again. Mistakes are bound to happen.

5. Work hard and play by the rules. Education is a must. Learn for the love of learning; you can learn from every experience. If you fail or lose, don't lose the lesson. The more you learn, the more doors will open.

6. Most important, never forget that true happiness comes only through the love and knowledge of our Lord and savior. What the world calls life's crossroads is actually a cross at the road, so be consoled. Your personal relationship with God will be the most stabilizing force in your life.

I may not possess all the answers, but the above ideas provide more than an adequate start.

Julie G. Williams

❖   ❖   ❖

December 14, 1998
Washington, DC

SUCCESS AIN'T SITTING STILL

I didn't finish high school but I was determined that, one day, I would earn my diploma. When I was small my sister and I worked hard to support our mother because our father deserted the family. I can remember working during the Depression for fifty cents a day. Times were tough but, thankfully, my story has a happy ending. I attended night school and eventually became a nurse. It took a lot of prayer and hard work. Today, when my children ask, "What is success?" I answer, "It ain't sitting still."

Quit crying and shuffling your feet. Show up, stand up, suit up, speak up, and fight the good fight!

Georgia Atkins

May 5, 2001
Marietta, GA

RESPECT ISN'T A QUALITY THAT
IS EASILY GRANTED. IT CAN
ONLY BE EARNED.

It's been brought to my attention that I am the oldest living graduate of
Spelman Seminary. It wasn't called Spelman College then, and as far as
I'm concerned I wish negroes would call my school by its proper name:
Spelman Seminary. I graduated in 1919 with degrees in education and
nursing. Now, I know what you're thinking. You're trying to guess my
age. Well, if you must know, I'm 102 years old. You can add it up. People are always asking, "Miss Rosalie, when are you going to retire?" I reply, "When I find something better to do. You may not find me in a
classroom but I'll still be teaching until the day I die!"

I love to learn. I relish the opportunity to acquire knowledge. I view
learning as a practical matter as well as spiritual. Yes, I am educated but
you will not find a string of letters at the end of my name. I am neither
physically gifted nor endowed with skills that call forth the famous or the
influential. I've never been invited to deliver a commencement address nor
have I ever written a letter of reference. I'm just a little black woman who
rolled with the punches. To be honest, regarding most matters I am only
average. If you examine my family, ex-slaves from Charleston, South Carolina, chances are you won't find anyone of note. There are no celebrities,
no doctors, lawyers, presidents, leaders of any sort—no one who could
be considered newsworthy. But, as Booker T. Washington told my class
when he visited our campus in 1918, "It is more important to live out
your values than to teach them."

I can remember every teacher who taught me—they were all white,
and not that it made a difference—as well as the names of my classmates
and every building on campus. I worked in the dining room and laundry

to pay my tuition. At the request of our founder, Miss Packard, Mr. Rosenwald traveled door-to-door throughout the south searching for young colored women with promise and who demonstrated strong Christian values. I tell you, every week when we marched into chapel, all three hundred strong, we looked like somebody. Dressed up, mind you and quite lovely. We conducted ourselves with the highest degree of grace and decorum. Our dresses—made in our home economics and industrial art classes—were lily white and smartly tailored, pressed with just a trace of starch. And heaven forbid if you were ever caught on campus or off with dull, unsightly shoes. You were a Spelman woman, which meant you looked your best from head to toe. My shoes were always polished. As I've always told my grandson, David, we had success on our mind. What was it, nearly eighty years ago? No matter how poor, our school and community had something going for it. It was all about hope. I don't care how desperate the moment. Folks used to say, "You may be down today but you're gonna be back up tomorrow." Back then our neighborhoods had stability. We all knew each other and, more important, we cared about each other. We knew who was living down the street, who completed their studies, and who got married. When there were trying times, we took it out in church. At the bottom of our difficulties was hope. There was no such thing as a hopeless person. No matter the barriers, regardless the obstacles, we never gave up hope. The other day, someone asked me about affirmative action and I felt the urge to share my mother's advice. My mama would hit a wall with her hand and say, "What do you see? A wall. Push hard and it becomes a door. Push harder and the door will open."

In spite of the difficulties of the day, we never stopped pushing. Spelman students were a group of sophisticated ladies instructed to set and achieve high standards, lofty goals. When it came to ambition we kicked it up a notch. Our instructors drilled in us, day in and day out, that ours would be the generation that would make a difference.

Yet this younger generation continues to struggle. Stripped of their childhood, they've seen and heard plenty. They struggle with discipline. They struggle with authority. They struggle with life, too often seeking style over substance. Always shaking their fist at God when they should be shaking His hand. Off the record, I seem to remember reading somewhere that since our race came to these shores more than three hundred years ago, this might be the first generation that has failed to move us forward. God has placed endless miracles and opportunities before them. This younger generation has been bathed in prosperity and by parents who wanted them to have better and easier lives. Here's a generation who has never known the bitter fruit of an economic depression or even a recession. They have never known separate and unequal or racial conflict. They have never known the ultimate sacrifice and commitment which only war can bring. Without any challenges or struggle they've become self-absorbed, confusing money with meaning, more with better, and wisdom with common sense. At a time when they could make a difference, many just want to make the news. As a result, many beg, blame, and sit around waiting for life to get worse. And guess what? It usually does. They claim their life is on course but I question where is it going.

And consider our young black males. "What are the odds," they ask, "of a black male making it in today's society?" I don't know. But one thing is for sure: The odds immediately begin to increase in your favor as soon as you remove that chip from your shoulder! The experts may have written you off, but I haven't. Society has labeled our children as the ungeneration: un-holy, un-grateful, and un-thankful. They get into gangs before they get into God; they get into crack before they get into church; and they frequently find violence before they find values. To make matters worse, they spend so much time being angry. Angry at this, angry at that. Unproductive precious time wasted in anger when they should really be thankful. I could go on, and will. I've tried to hold my tongue but it would only make the taste in my mouth even worse.

I was a small child during the Depression, the most severe in recent memory. I remember well when dinner was nothing more than grits and gravy. There was relief food available from the government, but many families, like mine, refused handouts. That's called pride. And, speaking of pride, here's my point: Young ladies—look at you—carrying on something awful! I'm shocked and appalled. I never thought I would see the day black women would wear outfits so earthy, so brazen, and so lewd. It breaks my heart to see our young women—I'm talking 'bout babies—dressed in some getup that would make a prostitute proud. They don't realize it's called Victoria's Secret for a reason. I don't know how it feels, but I can tell you how it looks, and I've got to ask: What is it that fascinates you about this mode of behavior? This question floats through my mind whenever I see adolescent girls at the mall, done up like some over-the-hill streetwalkers. What pains me is not that fourteen-year-old girls want to wear tight sweaters and show their pierced navels to boys. My anguish comes from the understanding that many of these young ladies walked past mothers and fathers on the way out the front door. Listen, children have always pushed the boundaries of acceptable dress, but it has been the duty of the parents, especially the father, to offer resistance. Sending your daughter back upstairs to change comes with the territory. So I say this with no joy—but certainly without apology. Do your job!

I know, I know. I'm old and set in my ways. But my patience has limits, and those limits are being tested. I'm past my time but, in my day, I was taught that all God-fearing women kept their knees close. Though it means the same thing, I still prefer the word expecting rather than pregnant, and, if you were said to be with child, you were immediately dismissed from school. Agree with me or not, but my sympathy abounds. I may not possess 20-20 vision but, spiritually, my eyesight is intact. I see a precious child who is unhappy. I see someone who is in pain. Do you really think I was born yesterday? I know the source of their hurt. A seductive outfit can't raise them up and a provocative tattoo won't change their condition. Shameful behavior won't drive away the depression. It's true: Sex may sell but it will sell your soul, too. Goodness knows this is a bit much to put on young minds, which may be why our children seem to be fourteen going on forty.

When I was young fast girls were called tramps, and boys who didn't respect women were said to be "on the make." And, speaking of our young men—Lord, have mercy! What do you expect from someone who has never heard "Boy, go get me a switch" and "Just wait until your father gets home." I swear, they're about to make me lose my religion.

Furthermore, heaven knows what Mother would've said if I came home speaking Ebonics let alone slang, using salty language, or refusing to do my best in school for fear of my peers saying I was "acting white." She would've slapped me silly. She got bent out of shape whenever you mismatched your subject and verb, or used improper diction. It hurts to even think about it. Mother had absolutely no tolerance for mediocrity or bad behavior. Let her tell it, it wasn't Christian-like. In our house a vulgar word always brought a swift reprimand. And, if you ever took the Lord's name in vain—child, you'd better duck! What's amazing is that, in spite of the discrimination and insensitivities of my day, I never knew of anyone in jail or in prison, homeless, begging on the street, or out of work. Most of my elders were short on education and opportunity, but long on caring and love, and they tried to live what they preached. I remember the shocked whispers when someone in the church was thought to be unfaithful to his wife or if a young girl and boy made a mistake and she got pregnant. I learned from my parents that marriage is a struggle and a sacred partnership between two people, and a covenant with God as well as the children the union brings into the world. So many times when I ask myself what in the world has happened to our families, all I can do is shrug.

Today, our youth talk so much about respect. Without rhyme or reason they insist upon it at all costs. They seem to be on a quest for fame and attention that knows no limits, even if it leads to ill-mannered, uncouth behavior. Killing each other like flies over the most minor slight. So much rage—even eye contact, in many cases, is seen as a threat. Their desire, however, is not hard to understand. They seek only what society has denied them for far too long—that is, to be somebody. Yet, even understanding all this, I can't pull myself to agree with their reasoning. If they only knew that the world does not operate in such a manner.

To these eyes, respect isn't a quality that is easily granted. It can only be earned. Respect is akin to honesty, truthfulness, humility, hard work, decency, discipline, pride, and, most important, responsibility. Respect, young lady and young man, comes by knowing the difference between right and wrong, and doing what you're supposed to do. It's a part of home training. Respect means that you are answerable for your behavior and you fully accept the consequences created by your actions. Respect means that you will not blame others for the conditions in your life. Why? Because blame carries guilt, and responsibility carries rewards. Blame is negative while responsibility propels you forward to a greater good. Blame never unites, it separates. Blame never smiles, it frowns. Blame never forgives, it rejects. And, blame never builds, it destroys. Responsibility and respect are key components of adulthood. If you haven't learned these lessons, it's not too late. Life will provide you with plenty of opportunities to get it right.

I don't want to harp on this matter, but I'm left with little choice. So, baby, do you really want respect? If so, let me give you a heaping helping: clean up your mess; mind your manners; keep your promise; take your feet off of the furniture and get rid of that attitude; bathe the children; hold down a job; buy her some flowers; tuck your child in at night; pay the phone bill; let me hear you say "It's my fault"; show some appreciation; stay out of trouble; teach your son, who worships the ground you walk on, how to tie a tie; wipe a runny nose; mix a formula and potty train your daughter; say your prayers; pull your pants up; take your hand off your hip; learn to communicate; do more than take up space; quit being so mealymouthed; and stand up and be counted! This is the quickest way to respect that I know. Do this, and not only will you be somebody, you'll have all the respect you can handle.

If I stepped on your toes, I'm sorry. Believe me, this is not my intention. But I've never been one to mince my words, and I'm not about to start now. I realize what I said might be painful, but some of you don't have the sense you were born with.

We're better than that or at least we should be,

Rosalie Andrews

✦   ✦   ✦

February 2001
Decatur, GA

YOU ARE A MIRACLE

To my children and grandchildren,

I hope my words will be of great value. There is a special influence that carries each of us to our final destination. To uncover yours you need only to look in the mirror. You are a living, breathing miracle! There is no need for you to imitate or emulate anyone. You need not be another Michael Jordan or Janet Jackson. There is no one like you, nor will there ever be anyone like you in this world or in the next. So just being you is more than enough. You are the salt of the earth, capable of moving mountains and performing the impossible. As a child of African American descent, your ancestry reads like a who's who of great personalities. You've got the blood of kings and queens flowing through your veins. The greatness of your past is the key to your future. Molded from dust by the hands of God Almighty, an offspring of the most high, you've been given the world and dominion over it. You are more than a human being, you are a human becoming.

You are a miracle. Ninety-eight point six degrees without breaking a sweat. Minute by minute, day after day, your heart beats six million times a year, giving oxygen to every muscle, nerve, and fiber in your body. No one has ever created a finer machine. You, granddaughter, have been blessed with the power to conceive, carry to term, and birth another human being. And you, grandson, as a loving and supportive copartner, you've been given the ability to plant a seed as well as the responsibility to guide, direct, and nurture your child.

You are such an inspiration. You surprise your critics and amaze your adversaries. You return good for evil, and love everybody, including your enemies. You survive everything that does not kill you. Your spirit can warm the lonely, uplift the hopeless, and encourage the defeated. Even when coping with pain and disappointment, you bend but you do not break. You hold everything together even when there is nothing to hold on to. You are fearfully and wonderfully made. You are heir of salvation and purchase of God; you are born of His spirit and washed in His blood.

So wipe your tears and dry your eyes. Never hide your talents, make light of your abilities, or bemoan your circumstances. At the moment of your birth, you cried while those around you smiled. I challenge you to live life in such a manner that the second you pass on to glory you'll be the one smiling and those around you will be catching tears. You are the greatest miracle in the world!

There's a logic in every journey,
Ann Harris

May 2000
Atlanta, GA

SING YOUR SONG

If the Lord has placed a song in your heart, it's best that you sing it. Your dreams will vanish in an instant if you fail to release your song. On their deathbed some people look back on their lives and are overwhelmed with a sense of failure. Their heart grows heavy as they reflect on how they squandered opportunities, took for granted precious relationships, neglected to find their true place, and shunned the importance of spiritual growth. Because they had left so much of their lives for later, their souls are burdened by unfulfilled dreams and a sense of incompleteness. They bear a lifetime of regrets. There is no need to leave this world full of remorse and sorrow. The world owes you nothing except the opportunity to succeed or fail. The ladders by which you may climb to attain your good fortune are all about you. But it is you who must do the climbing. The Lord may point the way, but you must push. So take your hands out of your pockets and release your song. When you look back over your life it should be a time of praise and thanksgiving. Tell your story. Shout it, share it, show it, live it, and sing it every day of your life! You've got only one life to live so don't live it on hold.

Sarah Reed

April 5, 2001
Atlanta, GA

NOT MY WILL BUT THY WILL BE DONE

I am flattered that someone would ask me to write a letter regarding my life experiences. Now who could possibly care about me and what I have done? I was told I could write whatever I so desired so I decided to discuss the one subject in which I seem worthy: Longevity. Now there's a word for you. If there's any one single theme that stands out in my life, it's longevity. It's hardly an easy march to walk through history but for the past century I've been doing just that. The good Lord has been kind enough to keep me around for one hundred years so I could bear witness to so many changes.

You talk about the gift of age—a lot can happen in one hundred years. I've buried my mother, father, ex-husband, and youngest son. But I've also been fortunate to see the births of my four grandchildren, eight great-grandchildren, and nine great-great-grandchildren. And yes, it's true, I had to lug the weight of an inferior education as well as the ball and chains of poverty and low self-esteem. However, as my Lord has assured me, when the prizes of life shall be awarded, the distance run, the handicaps I was forced to bear, and the burdens that were placed upon me will all be taken into account.

Most of us have been given many more blessings than we care to acknowledge. Over the course of my life I've seen my fair share of U.S. Presidents—nineteen to be exact—come and go. I was born when McKinley was in office, and, though I received a wonderful letter from President Clinton wishing me the best on my 101st birthday, FDR remains my favorite. He gave us social security. They say Roosevelt was a rich man's son, but heaven knows, he sure did a lot for poor folks.

These old eyes have seen plenty, the good and the bad. I have personally witnessed Jim Crow, backbreaking labor, and the type of treatment of one race by another that would make a weak man question his faith. I was well into my sixties before I could vote or eat in a white-owned restaurant. If I ever got hungry and was tempted to eat out, I had to sit in the kitchen with the rest of the help. I have also seen the civil rights movement and the Montgomery bus boycott. To tell you the truth, when I was told what Rosa Parks did and that I no longer needed to ride in the back of the bus, it took me weeks before I got the nerve to sit up front. I just walked to the back by habit. I guess this was one of those things that had to grow on you. Through it all, I can proudly say no matter the injustice or the indignity, I refused to be scathed by bitterness. I would not allow the insensitivity of another to turn my heart cold.

Longevity: That's a word you don't hear too often. I've seen this country go from horse and buggy to car and train to airplanes to landing an astronaut on the moon. When I was growing up hardly anyone had a telephone or a bathtub in their home. And, if you ever saw a car, that was a big deal. There were no paved roads. I remember what life was like before television and talk radio; before penicillin, polio shots, microwave ovens, frozen foods, light beer, Xerox copies, and drug rehabilitation. I can recall life before gangs, school shootings, burglar bars on windows, metal detectors, crack houses. I can remember when there was no black on black crime (we never had to lock our front door), before cussing was allowed on television, and before prayer was removed from public schools. In my day the teacher was always right. I can recall a time before rampant divorce, teenage pregnancy, and the word "shacking." In my day you got married first, then lived together. How quaint. I remember those days well. So many pleasures that we enjoy today had not been invented. The American flag held only forty-five stars. Arizona, Oklahoma, New Mexico, Alaska, and Hawaii had yet to be deemed states. At that time, I was told the Eiffel Tower was the tallest structure in the world. If I got sick, two teaspoons of Castor oil would get me back on my feet in no time. And, it would be years before I could buy Coca-Cola, my favorite drink. Back in those days a bottle cost only a nickel. When I look back, I guess I've come a long way, indeed.

As bad as it may sound, please don't look at me as someone special. I may have made a few sacrifices during my day but certainly no heroics. I read somewhere that the first eighty years of life are the hardest. If you make it to your eighties, everyone is surprised that you're still alive. But if you live to see a hundred, well that's something else. Folks treat you with respect just for living so long. In my book age is nothing but a number. Just because you reach a certain number doesn't mean that you give up living. Look at me, I like to bowl. I'm active in my church and I sing in three choirs. I love to travel—I've been to Hawaii, Mexico, and the Virgin Islands. I guess because I grew up in the country I still piddle in my garden. And I'm an officer in my neighborhood association. I make sure our children stay off the corner and go to school. As long as you're living, you're youthful. Youth is not a time of life, but a state of mind. Years may wrinkle the skin, but to stumble around without hope and enthusiasm, the spice of life, that will wrinkle your soul. Fullness of life is not measured in years alone. Nobody grows old merely by the coming and going of birthdays. You grow old by giving up your hopes and dreams. When it comes to life there's a starting point, a finish line, and dreams in between.

How did I make it this long? I'm still asking myself that question. To tell you a bit about who I am, I was born March 7, 1900 in Barnett, Georgia, just up the way from Crawfordville. Nothing more than the crossing of two dirt roads, Barnett doesn't exist anymore. Though I've never been one to speak of hardship, as a child it seems that's all I ever knew. When I was five years old my mother passed, and Father died two years later. I was raised by aunt who removed me from school after the third grade. Three miles from our farm stood a one-room shotgun house where I attended school. This little room was complete with stools, benches, a handful of students, and a potbelly stove. They said my teacher, Mr. Stone, taught grades one through six although no one ever knew anyone to make it as far as the sixth grade. Mr. Stone would stand near the blackboard with a book in one hand and a switch in the other. And if you didn't know your lesson, well shame on you. He was nice but firm. During the winter months he had to rotate us, moving those children in the back of the classroom up front near the stove before we froze. With Spring came mild weather as well as crops and planting. Back then, colored children could only attend school three months out of the year—January through March. When I was eight my aunt said my hands would be better suited if they were hitched to a plow and wagon rather than toting school books. My school days and dreams of becoming a teacher were lost, forever.

At sixteen I married Boisié Gunn, a young man who lived with his grandparents on a neighboring farm. We never courted. My aunt was impressed with what he had, with his horses and cows and whatnot. He seemed like a nice man but, to be honest, our marriage never took root. We settled down in Crawfordville, not too far from Augusta. It wasn't long before we started a family. Fred, my oldest son, was born in 1916, and my second child, Raymond, in 1918. A few years later, when the boll weevil ate its way through cotton farms throughout the South, we were forced to give up farming and move to Atlanta.

Almost immediately, upon arriving in Atlanta, I worked as a domestic in the homes of white families. They weren't rich people, they were just good livers. I raised a total of eleven white children from birth to adolescence, changing diapers, washing clothes, cooking meals, and serving as a constant companion. I earned a dollar a day. More than once, one of my white babies would say, "Nana, you're more like my mama than my real mama." I loved all my children. We seemed to lose touch when the last family I worked for moved to North Georgia.

By far the toughest day of the week was Wednesday—wash day. I would start bright and early by building a fire beneath a number two tub. Then, I would soak, wash, and boil bundles of clothes. Minutes later, I would stir the tub with a stick before rinsing and wringing out each piece by hand. After hanging each batch on the line, I would iron all day long, pressing razor-sharp creases onto every pillow case, sheet, pants, and shirt. I swear, when I got through my little fingers looked like prunes. I worked twelve-hour days—seven days a week—many times staying overnight, catching the "Soldiers Home" bus at five-thirty in the morning and arriving home near eight at night. I barely had enough energy to go home, get my own children squared away, and start all over again the following morning. Overworked and under rested, seems like I would go to bed tired and get up tired. Sundays were best, however. I would get off work just in time to attend the 3 p.m. church service. I worked well into my seventies before I decided to call it quits.

Well, that's the story of my life. But enough about me. What about you? What dreams and hopes does your heart hold? Are you taking advantage of the many opportunities I couldn't even imagine? Are you realizing your full potential? That's the question that rests before our younger generation. You're not here to look good or to take up space. Are you stepping out and stepping up into the life you were meant to live? Do you do your best? Do you give it all you've got? You can always push harder, strive higher. Do you honor your mother and father? How about saying your prayers, minding your manners, and going to church? Have you asked the Almighty why He has kept you around so long? I know I have. Do you abide by the Golden Rule? Do you look for the best in others? If it's true that the good Lord does keep books, what will be written about you? Will it acknowledge your character and contribution? Will your example be a gentle reminder of what life is all about? Do you laugh often and love much? Are you willing to forgive and forget? Can you look me square in the eye and say, "Not my will but Thy will be done?" Folks never get tired of asking, "How in the world did I make it all these years?" Well, if you can allow His will to be done, Child, you've already found the key.

Maybe I'm a teacher, after all,

Annie Gunn

❖   ❖   ❖

April 19, 2000
Indianapolis, IN

WHAT YOU CALL NO CHANCE, MAY BE YOUR ONLY CHANCE

There's a belief I now know to be true: One, living entails a series of highs and lows. And two, you gain nothing by attempting to skirt life's challenges. There's always something you can do no matter how difficult the course, how tough the moment. Living without goals and dreams can be both limiting and draining. Somehow you must drum up the courage to pursue your life's calling. Playing it small, shrinking from the fight doesn't serve anyone's purpose. Each of us dreams of success, and everyone wants to be a winner. In due time you, too, will succeed once you get your mind and thoughts in order; once you cancel your pity party and get off your blessed assurance and stop seeking reasons to quit. To accept failure as final means to finally accept failure. And, if you have yet to realize your calling, to pursue your highest good, maybe that's why you've been created—to uncover your life's work. There's nothing so pitiful as an individual who has acres of land, but not an inch of ambition; someone with so much to live for, surrounded by opportunity at every turn, but walking on a treadmill going nowhere; someone whose wealth can be counted in millions, but whose life sinks into insignificance. Ignoring your talents and gifts is like dying a slow death. You must find a purpose that excites you like no other; a dream or cause which you are called to defend and pursue with all abandon. Only then will you be happy, only then will you stand in the winner's circle of life.

So take my advice: Listen to the mustn'ts, listen to the don'ts, listen to the shouldn'ts and the can'ts, listen to the never haves, then listen closely—anything is possible. You were born to win. You are a child of God born to glorify His power. Don't wait for your place to be made for you—make it yourself! Don't wait for someone to give you a lift—lift yourself. Many times, the best thing that can happen is to be tossed overboard into a sea of chaos and confusion and compelled to swim. What you call no chance, may be your only chance.

Lenora Grissom

❖   ❖   ❖

February 25, 1999
Brooklyn, NY

A GOOD EXAMPLE IS THE BEST SERMON YOU CAN PREACH

You are my first grandchild. I am so proud of you, and I cannot help but think of all the good things that you are doing to make yourself into a fine, young lady. I am glad that you are in college and keeping yourself busy. I know that it hasn't been easy, but if you study hard, it will all pay off in the end.

Though our family has never been wealthy, we've been lucky. Somehow we learned the value of an education. Your great-grandfather and grandmother preached honesty, fairness, charity, faith in God, and to acquire as much education as possible. You come from a family of farmers who knew nothing but dirt and hard work. Your great-grandmother Lucy, however, made only one exception to working the land, and that was to go to school. "An education," she would say, "is the one thing that can never be taken from you." There has never been a truer statement.

I hope that I have been a worthy role model. I know that a good example is the best sermon you can preach. I've dreamed of the day that I could pass on to you all that I know. I have searched high and low, near and far for the one piece of advice that could make your life more meaningful. I've searched everywhere. I looked in the world, but could not find it. I looked in books, but could not find it there, either. Finally, I turned within and found both the source of happiness as well as the cure to despair. And now, I offer it to you. I know you're ready to accept it: Never give up on life, and share your heart with others. It is in life and love that you will be richly blessed. I am always here for you.

Thelma Bartholomew

❖　　❖　　❖

May 14, 2001
Atlanta, GA

ONCE A TEACHER, ALWAYS A TEACHER

I graduated from Spelman College in 1929, and I taught school for more than forty years. I don't think much about the past ninety-four years, but when I do I know I've got one last stop to make, so I dare not waste time. I guess that's been my rule of life. We don't have time to whine and complain; to be bitter, resentful or jealous; to backstab one another or to pick each other apart. Nor is there time for you to say, "I can't do this or I can't do that," or to give up on your dreams. During my years in the classroom, this is all I ever asked of my students:

(1) Bloom where you are planted and stick to the task at hand. Attitude makes all the difference in the world.
(2) Hold tight to your values. Value yourself and treat others with respect.
(3) Never confuse money with success. To be master of your destiny is the greatest reward.

When I go on to glory I don't want folks to say "Oh, she was okay," or "She was a kind ol' lady." Rather, I want people to mention what is truly important. At my funeral I would like to look down and see a celebration of life. A celebration where stories are told and praise rings out; where a few tears are shed; and where everyone in attendance realizes here lies a special person who made a difference. Wouldn't that be something! Yes, my speech is slurred; my hearing may be bad; my legs are somewhat useless; and my eyesight has grown dim; but my words and thoughts are as sharp as ever.

Once a teacher, always a teacher,
Zimmie Shelton

❧   ❧   ❧

August 23, 2001
Washington, DC

WHAT IS LIFE?

I've been asked the question, "If I had the opportunity, what would I tell my grandchild about life?" Here is a subject in which I feel quite comfortable. When it comes to living, I feel I am well versed. I guess it comes with the territory. It takes many years to learn the role of a grandmother. It's nothing you can train for, usually the title is handed to you when you've been looking the other way. When you read our letters I imagine the story is the same: Born black and female during a time when it paid to be neither. Raised in obscurity, and underestimated from day one. Poverty could've swallowed us whole the way it swallows most, but we wouldn't allow it. We were never educated enough, never influential enough, never wealthy enough, and never talented enough. But for all our nevers, we've been more than enough for any slight or stumbling block society could heave our way. We are the women who took rotten apples and made the best cobbler. We took rags and frayed pieces of clothing and made handsome quilts. Each time we were given less, we transformed it into more. Of heartbreak and despair, we've known more than most but somehow we managed to survive intact. Tears may roll down our cheeks and we may throw up our hands in disgust, but as long as we can whisper "Praise God," all is right in our world. When you come to write our life story, it can be encapsulated in one word: survival.

Like so many black grandmothers, mine is a life of commitment and survival, and too much to do. In my day, life was not a journey for the weak or the fainthearted. From the word go, I've learned firsthand the fine art of prevailing. Now my attention is turned to you. "What is life?" you ask. How can I explain the wonder of life in terms that you will understand? My Webster's Dictionary defines life as "a series of phases; a gift from God; the period from birth to death; a way or manner of living; survival." According to this definition, if we put all the phases together the entire experience would be called life. But with all due respect to Mr. Webster, I feel the best way to define life is to simply look within.

From the moment the doctor slapped you on your little bottom, your life was set in motion. Your initial cry was the sweetest sound your mother and father heard in a long time. From there, life would take its course. You loved life from the moment you took your first breath, especially all of the attention thrown your way—the holding, the petting, the feedings, the toys, the beautiful colors in your crib—not to mention your security blanket that you dragged everywhere. The long rides in your stroller in the middle of the day were quite enjoyable, too. The gentle rain that fell upon the pane outside your bedroom window was a sure sign that you would soon be fast asleep. You were so young and precious—you still are. This phase of your life could be called your growing years.

But life is never a bed of roses. If memory serves me right, you were only two when your mother and father divorced. I call it your season of discontent. Even at that age you were sad and confused. Your disruptive behavior was followed by the questions, "Why? Why doesn't Daddy come by? Why is Mommy crying? Why doesn't anybody love me?" During this phase your little spirit seemed troubled. But such is life. Years would go by before you and your Dad would begin to restore your relationship. Though you were getting older, you appeared well adjusted. Several of your childhood friends responded to similar circumstances with resentment and hostility. But you were shielded by three strong black women—your mother, Aunt Dolly, and me, your grandmother— who were determined, with God's help, to nestle you in a loving, nurturing environment. Your Mom took you on vacations, fun places: Universal Studios, Miami Beach, and Los Angeles, California. You spent a few weeks each summer with family and friends. You even came to see me in Oklahoma City, Oklahoma—1,100 miles away—for your first visit to the country. There, you found the pace of life much slower. There was ample time to visit the zoo, fly kites, and picnic at the lake. I remember how we claimed a huge rock as ours by writing our names and the date upon it. You rode horses, caught turtles, fished for catfish, and fed chickens. You even learned to whittle, a skill your friends back in Washington, D.C., know little. I taught you how to experience natural fun—pleasure and enjoyment without television or video games. And how you loved to hear the stories of my childhood. You sat with your chin in your hands as I relived the times my father would treat me and my sister to the fair, and buy each of us all the cotton candy and candied apples we could eat.

You sat motionless when I recounted how my father would buy ice cream for every child in our neighborhood. Because of segregation, blacks weren't served within any restaurant. Therefore, Father would inform the owner as to his intentions and bring out ice cream two cones at a time. If the choice were yours you seemed more than willing to put up with the humiliation of segregation if it meant sitting on a curb with your buddies to enjoy a scoop or two.

At some point, you told your mother that you would like to live in Oklahoma. She wasn't a bit surprised. I believe the experiences we shared were special. These were moments that get lost in the midst of the inner city, complete with its hectic schedules and fast-paced lifestyles. I know you need the youth and vitality of your mother but you also need my slower pace full of values and timeless truths that will provide the foundation for a full and rewarding childhood.

I guess you could call the latest phase of your life learning years. You've learned to be a better student. Without a proper education life will be difficult at best. You learned to be patient and communicate with others. You've learned that life is a special gift where too few of us remove the wrapping. You've learned that your circumstances will get better only when you get better. And you will get better providing you allow yourself to be guided by God's love and embrace the teaching and values of your elders. Over the course of my life I've tried to be a steadfast soul, a loving and caring wife, a faithful mother, a patient grandmother, and a valued prayer partner. I am a caretaker of an era gone by. Someone who makes every child her child. In spite of my own pain, in spite of my own suffering, even in the midst of whatever problems I was going through, I sought to make your life a bit more comfortable. And though I've never enjoyed the status nor the financial rewards that accompany success—at least by the world's standards—I've experienced the riches of the mind and spirit. My only desire is to place this torch of wisdom into your hands and light the way for a meaningful life. As I look over your shoulder I believe I have succeeded. You cannot determine how you come into this world, but you can certainly decide how you leave it.

With more hope and love than you'll ever know,
Dolly C. Turner

❧   ❧   ❧

October 17, 1998
Yazoo City, MS

BY THIS GUIDING LIGHT

My Dear Grandchildren:

As we enter the new millennium, it is a privilege for me to pass on to each of you guiding principles that will help you cope with life's unexpected twists and turns. As a woman who has spent the bulk of her time (seventy years) in the twentieth century, I believe I possess more than enough wisdom to share with you. Life will offer the bitter and the sweet, and you must be able to cope with both. Life will not always be easy; in fact, many times it can be downright hard. Just think about it: It's hard to show love and caring when people say hateful things. It's hard to help only a few when you want to share your heart with so many. But remember, Almighty God will never leave you. Those of my generation faced many barriers as you will, and now do. Nonetheless, you must put forth every effort to succeed.

To do so you must prepare yourself; respect authority; maintain your self-esteem; keep a mind of your own; work for an honest living; never be overtaken by your peers; avoid drugs; be not anxious for anything; and keep in mind that family will always be there for you. Furthermore, be strong and of good courage; fear not, it is the Lord your God who goes with you. The task ahead of you is never as great as the power behind you. God doesn't call the qualified; He qualifies the called. Our Father will not forsake you. No one is too lost to be found, too low to be lifted. You've got to remember who you are and who you belong to. Your love must know no barrier, and you must embrace the type of courage that cannot be shaken, a faith strong enough for the darkness, a strength sufficient for any task, and grace to meet life's challenges. By this guiding light I have lived and now pass the light on to you. It's been a great journey . . .

Your stumbling blocks have been brushed aside, your path is clear,

Catherine J. Brent

◈   ◈   ◈

November 17, 1998
Opalocka, FL

DON'T ALLOW THE TRAPPINGS OF LIFE TO DISTRACT YOU FROM THE MEANING OF LIFE

I have no way of knowing whether you will read my letter. It doesn't matter. What does matter, however, is that I've touched a life or made a difference. If you make life better for others, you will be worthy of the same.

I thank God for my childhood, in spite of the hard times. My parents shared their love and taught me the true riches of life. We spent time in family prayer learning Bible verses, and saving for the future. As a child, I watched my mother and father label three glass jars "tithes," "bills," and "food" and drop coins into each. Sometimes it would only be a few dimes, a nickel or two, or a pile of pennies but, regardless of the amount, they would give thanks. As long as I can remember, my family was only a day's march ahead of poverty. But don't get me wrong. We weren't poor, we just had empty pockets. Mother would always say, "If there is a will, there's a way." Well, she was right. From these three little jars my parents not only managed to buy a new home, but they saved enough money to send five of their seven children to college—myself included!

We are told in scripture to seek life's greater gifts. Don't let the trappings of life distract you from the meaning of life. Don't spend time searching for happiness. Happiness, in turn, will find you. Cars, houses, bank accounts—none of these items mean a thing. Rather, seek peace, contentment, and fulfillment. These will last you forever. When all is said and done, any honor we receive will come from how we served, not how we were served. It's the journey there, not the arrival.

Prayerfully submitted,
Gladys McClain

✦   ✦   ✦

A FINAL WORD OR TWO ON THE GREATEST OF ALL STATEMENTS

March 1999
Milwaukee, WI

Listen. You can change your condition. Though our world, with its cold hands, seems to be blocking your path, hold your head high. Happiness and fulfillment are not destinations waiting your arrival but the manner in which you travel. Life is a game in which the score that matters most is not determined by wins or losses but by doing the best you can with what you've been given.

Yvonne D. Greer

March 3, 1998
Pittsburgh, PA

It's not what others say about you; it's what you believe about yourself.
Measure your possibilities not according to what you see in yourself, but
according to what the Lord sees in you. It's better to look ahead and prepare than to look back and regret. Go anywhere, provided it's forward.
You are the promise, the pride, those who will change our world for the
better. Now is your time. Take it on.

Laura Justice Moss

❖   ❖   ❖

April 1999
New York, NY

Whether you're the front runner in this game called life or if you're
bringing up the rear, when you run this race you're gonna get tired. And
there were times when I grew tired. Tired of needing determination to
accomplish life's most basic tasks. Tired of folks taking me for granted.
Tired of being forced to work harder than other people. Tired of things
taking longer and costing more. And, basically, just plain tired. But I
tried my best not to allow my feelings to cloud my day. What do you do
after you recover from whatever it is that has set you back? My Bible tells
me that we are to live life "more abundantly." In other words, plant your
roots deep into your soul. In this race victory does not always belong to
the swift, nor do the spoils go to the strong. Place alone does not determine the prize. We must take into account the burdens that have been
endured.

Ethel Moore

March 17, 1998
Shelbyville, TN

If you believe this world owes you a living, you're wrong. In this game of life, you will receive few perks. You will be given no rest periods, free lunches, or special privileges. Thankfully, the rules were written in this manner. Life owes you the chance to be somebody, and nothing more. Plan on working and scraping for everything you get.

                                        Gladys Young Flack

Chapter Two

Live
This Day

hat could you do or accomplish if you really decided to step up and stand out, to really live this day? So many of us mistakenly believe that life's greatest tragedy is death or dying. As you will read, these grandmothers beg to differ. No, life's greatest tragedy is not the end of life but merely unfulfilled potential. In other words, to possess a talent or gift and not use it; to possess an ability that never blossoms; to be blessed with special qualities that fail to bloom.

So many of us underestimate our potential for growth and achievement. Our faces tells the story. We've allowed our past to impoverish us spiritually and emotionally. And, when questioned about our performance or the lack thereof, we give every excuse in the book. Mistakenly, we blame everything and everybody. We blame society, as well as our family and friends. Try as we may to shift the blame, what it all boils down to is us—YOU and ME!

We've lived in our skin so long, we tend to take ourselves and our capabilities for granted. However, we can and must change. Now, I am not implying that you reach for the moon, although that has already been accomplished. However, what I am suggesting is that you step back, close your eyes, and envision what you could become if you lived up to your potential and fully utilized this day.

Fulfilling your potential is not a choice; it is your divine obligation. Living this day is not what you have done. What you've done is history. Your yesterdays are not nearly as important as your tomorrows. Many destroy their potential by living in the glow of some shining moment in the past. One of life's most disturbing pictures is that of a man or woman with faded dreams, lost aims; someone who made little or no effort to continue their struggle forward. In short, an individual who began with bright prospects but who allowed his or her hopes to become dead and dull. Men and women who have permitted their stan-

dards to drop, their ambitions to sag, their enthusiasm to cool under life's daily grind, and who have died a slow death with their music trapped in them.

Listen closely. You will despise yourself later if you look back on life and realize that you possessed the talent and the ability to accomplish bold dreams but couldn't muster the courage to try. When I think of people who failed to live this day, I see children who are hurting; I see men and women caught in a web of despair; I see tears instead of laughter; I see lives filled with bitterness and self-pity. We are only a mere shell of what we could become because we fail to realize our true potential and live this day. Your potential is the business that you could do but haven't done. Your potential is the grade you could earn but haven't made. Your potential is the promotion you could receive and have yet to attain. Your potential is the parent that you could be but have yet to become. The ladders by which you may climb to attain your good fortune are all about you. But it is you who must do the climbing. Fate and opportunity may point the way, but you must push. As the old folks used to say, "The Lord gives every bird its food, but He doesn't throw it into the nest." The past is history; tomorrow is a mystery. Today is a gift; that's why it's called the present. All power has been vested in you. Now take your hands out of your pockets and live this day!

❀   ❀   ❀

June 19, 2000
New York, NY

JUMP FEETFIRST INTO LIFE AND PARTICIPATE

As anyone who has ever achieved the impossible can tell you, to move forward you've got to step out and do or say something that may make zero sense to everyone but you. Some folks will claim you're taking a leap of faith or that you've lost your mind. But only rarely are you forced to jump blindly. By first turning a goal or an obstacle inside out—looking at it from every possible angle—you'll recognize that what you can do far outweighs what you can't. And armed with that knowledge, you'll discover that taking a risk doesn't feel quite so risky.

When I retired as a domestic at age seventy, for the first time in my life I had an abundance of time on my hands. I worked hard my entire life. This should come as no surprise. After all, when your great-great-grandparents are sold into slavery for a combined fifty cents; when a bucket is indoor plumbing and tree stumps your furniture; when your father works one shift as a highway worker and another in the fields on a family farm in Phillips, South Carolina, just to make ends meet; when you're one of a handful of children raised with love but in near poverty; when nobody thought you'd be anything but a country bumpkin pulling down a minimum wage, then you don't acknowledge the difficulties or the sweat. You keep the pain inside where it pushes you toward greatness. Somehow you've got to turn pain into power and find the heart to live.

When I joined the New York Road Runners Club nearly twenty years ago, I didn't intend to run any races. I only wanted to be a volunteer, someone who stands on the sidelines and hands water to those who run by. It took me several years of volunteering and watching races before I got the nerve to enter my first 5-K. I was scared, but I finished—and not in last place, either. It was the first time in my life I did something just for me.

In 1998, I took an even bigger plunge. I decided to run the New York City Marathon. I was seventy-six years old. My buddies at the Road Runners Club kept prodding me. "Miss Singleton," they insisted, "you should run the marathon." I thought they were nuts. I replied, "Child, if you knew how many floors these knees have scrubbed, and how many steps these ankles have climbed." But they persisted. It wasn't long before I finally caved in. Once I decided to run I began training. Every morning at 5 a.m. sharp—rain or shine—I would step outside of my New York City apartment and run three to four miles. I kept up this routine for weeks on end. When word got around as to what I was attempting to do, those who knew me questioned my sanity. Everyone wanted to know why in the world was I running. But nothing or no one was going to deter me. When race day finally arrived, I was more than prepared. Though my legs may have been shaky, my will and determination were like the rock of Gibraltar. When I took off from the starting line and witnessed the sea of runners and endless miles before me, I said to myself, "Lord have mercy. It's gonna be a long way home." You don't run the marathon— you survive it! So many times people make a commitment, then real life shows up. Like so many, I've been the ultimate spectator. Now was the time for me to jump feetfirst into life and participate.

Regardless of where life may find you, you can live more vibrantly, more meaningfully. Each of us possesses the potential to do better. Wherever you are, I challenge you to dream and hope. Use hope and imagination as weapons of survival. If money is tight, dream of the day when your ship comes in. If you're addicted, dream of the day in which you will be drug free. If you're facedown in the gutter, dream of the day when you will be on your feet. Yes, you must face your circumstances as they are but never stop dreaming of how things ought to be. There is something in you greater than that which is holding you back, which is withholding your good, and thwarting your dreams. There is something in you that is more powerful than any cruel fate, mightier than anything that could mar your future—a force that is independent of hard times and hard luck; an energy that can rise above sickness, above pain, above any and every thing that would hinder you from becoming the man or woman the Creator intends for you to be. God Almighty gave you the greatest power any individual could possess. He gave you the power to love, the power to laugh, the power to pray, the power to choose, the power to dream, and the power to hope against hope.

To play it safe is not to play,
Lucille Singleton

March 9, 2000
Cincinnati, OH

WITH ALL THY GETTING

Dearest Daughter,

I have lived a good life. I've followed my path and I carry few regrets. My dreams, though some would be labeled insignificant, were kept in sight. Whether large or small, they were my dreams. If I could offer you a few suggestions for living, my advice would include the following: The world is a wonderful place and you've got a right to be here. Never undermine your worth by comparing yourself to others. You are nature's greatest miracle, a designer original, perfect in every way. You've been blessed with talents and abilities. God has created you in a manner that cannot and will not be duplicated. He bestowed upon you qualities and gifts that only you can express. Since the beginning of time there has never been nor will there ever be anyone who can walk, talk, and move exactly like you. Your personality and features are different from anyone else—past or present. It's time to take stock. You are nature's greatest miracle.

Who else has done what you've done? Survived what you've faced? Name another who has managed to withstand all that you've confronted. Never bury or conceal your gifts. Never underestimate your talents. Never settle for the crumbs of life! Settling for anything less than you desire or know you deserve leads to betrayal. When you disown or discount your inner qualities so, too, does your world, including those you hope to share your life with. Be proud. You have much to celebrate. You've beaten the odds. Proclaim your existence!

Never gauge success by the world's standards. Fancy cars and fine clothes may be fun to own, but they've never added up to a meaningful life or contributed to a lasting legacy. There's something that will last long after your journey ends. It's the love you've bestowed on others.

After you're gone, no one will recall that you wore the finest suits or splashed on the most expensive cologne. We spend the first fifty years of our life satisfying our ego, and our remaining years trying to clean our slate. Therefore, waste little time and effort searching for peace and contentment in a material world. The world may value appearances, but I am more concerned with gifts from the heart. Ultimately our goal as believers should not be how wealthy we can be but how well we can be. Success means more than money. Plenty of folks with nothing in their pockets, and thousands more without even a pocket, are wealthy. You are rich or poor according to what you are, not what you own. Penniless is not poverty and ownership does not mean possession.

Be grateful for your blessings and share with those less fortunate. Blessings are based on God's grace, not on merit. If you've got fine cars, fancy clothes, and a nice home, I'm happy for you. But every privilege brings responsibility. Status and income may keep you living, but only your ideals will keep you alive. Don't run through life so fast that you not only forget where you've been, but also where you're going. Take time to enjoy the world by soaking in life's little pleasures. By living your life one day at a time, you'll live all the days of your life. The best that life has to offer is free, and lies openly at your doorstep: a colorful garden, a setting sun, a moonlit sky, a kiss good-bye, and the smile of a child. You've been blessed by a loving God with an abundant world. If you would only take the time to embrace it. Before you take inventory of what you've lost, take a long, hard look at what you've gained. Plain living, honest effort, and higher thought will help to uncover life's true riches. Measure every stage of your life with the yardstick of appreciation and humility. There is something better than putting money into your pocket, and that is putting beauty and love into your heart. Trust in my words and you will never be poor.

In closing, hold fast to your dreams and stay the course. Never give up when you still have something to give. Though friends during times of tribulation may disappoint, search for that inner voice and be prepared to listen. Make this day better than all others. Just for today appreciate the next twenty-four hours and try not to tackle all of your problems at once. Just for today walk tall and smile more. Don't be afraid to say "I love you." Just for today uplift your mind and learn something new. With all thy getting, get understanding. Just for today take the high road; do the right thing. Read something inspirational and strengthen your spirit in the process. Just for today find fault with no one. Look for the best in every living soul. Contact an old neglected friend. Release ill feelings. Let go of an old grudge. It could provide someone with a badly needed lift. Just for today apologize when you are wrong. Just for today take a risk; vow to do something that you always wanted to do. You can grow, right here, right now. Embrace every opportunity that may provide a better life for you and your family. Your reward will come if you step out on faith. Just for today encourage a child to do his or her best. Our youth need sturdy shoulders to lean on more than they need critics. Just for today take care of yourself. Remember, you're all you've got. Finally, just for today thank the Lord for the gift of life. Let this day be a reflection of the strength that resides within you; of the courage that lights your path; of the wisdom that guides your steps; and of the serenity that will be yours when this day has passed. You might have wasted yesterday; you may even be wasting today. But you will not waste tomorrow, for it has yet to come.

Run your own race, and keep the faith,
Jeannie Rogers

December 12, 1998
Hampton, VA

TODAY IS WHERE YOUR FUTURE BEGINS

Happiness. What is it? Happiness won't come to you. You, in turn, must go to it. And the place to start is within. You realize the cards that you are dealt are less important than the way you play your hand. When it comes to being happy there are many roads that you can travel. One path may lead to your dreams whereas another may end in sorrow and hardship. For some, happiness is power and prestige. To others, it can be found in a cozy home, a nice car, or the chance to catch up on overdue bills. But I've learned that true happiness is a bit more. Very little is needed to make a life happy. To me, happiness is good health and a sound mind. Happiness is being your own best friend, giving and sharing of yourself, and being content with life. Happiness is a grateful heart. It's the ability to see the splendor of the Fall; to hear the bells of Christmas; to anticipate the coming of Spring; and to feel the warmth and cool shade of Summer. Happiness is thankfulness: thankful for meaningful work, and the ability to lie down at night and awake to a brand new day. Finally, happiness is love: sharing your love and receiving another's love in return. The happiness you experience will be in direct proportion to the love you have shared. These feelings spell happiness. No one can make you happy or unhappy. Unhappiness is not knowing what you want out of life and then struggling to possess it. More overwhelming than contentment, happiness is the ultimate expression of joy and gratitude. It's what fills you up and fills you out. If you are holding anyone else accountable for your happiness, you're wasting time. Yesterday is only a dream, and tomorrow is but a vision. Therefore, look forward to this one day, for it alone is life. Tomorrow? You can do nothing until the sun rises again. Today, right now, is all the life there is. All you possess is the hour at hand. The time to be happy is now. The place to be happy is here. The way to be happy is to accept life as a blessed gift. After all, if you can't be happy what else is there?

Today is where your future begins,
Maude Hinton

❖   ❖   ❖

December 8, 1998
Chicago, IL

SNATCH THE SECONDS OF THE DAY AS IF YOU ONLY HAD THIS DAY TO LIVE

As a grandmother of three here are the words of wisdom I wish to share with you, our future.

You have finally reached the point in your young life when you answer only to yourself. Sounds wonderful, doesn't it? Or is it a bit frightening? Perhaps it helps to know the truth. The road of life brings many unexpected twists and turns. It is during these moments that you must stand strong. You may be disappointed if you fail but you are doomed if you don't try. A bend in the road does not mean the end of the road.

Discipline sets the tone for every avenue you travel. You can pay now, or you can pay later. But one way or another you will pay a price for all that you receive in terms of discipline. When I was a child I was so eager to move from one phase of my life to another. Now, I know better. Take it slow. Life should not be fleeting. Everything happens in its own time. Your life should be rich, meaningful, and rewarding. Take time to listen to your heart.

Be honest in all your dealings. It takes a lifetime to build a good name but one silly mistake to ruin one. Everything you think, say, or do is important. Be true to yourself and the principles you've been taught. What-over thoughts or acts you entertain—good or bad—will surely surface in your life. Therefore, "whatever things are true, whatever things are noble, whatever things are just, whatever things are pure, and of good report, think on these things" [Philippians 4:8]. Trust the God spirit and watch what it brings. Go out and snatch the seconds of the day as if you only had this day to live.

Don't just live your life, savor it . . .
Yvette Ridley

❖   ❖   ❖

September 20, 2000
Decatur, GA

LIVE YOUR DASH

A grandmother's wisdom, you ask? Not hard for me at all. I've grown up, grown old, and worshiped my God. Now my children are grown. I feel sadness for what was, but joy for what remains. The house is empty but my heart is full. My sole purpose is to offer you the chance to give your days on earth more meaning and fulfillment. I learned long ago that I shall venture through this world but once. Any good that I can do, or any kindness that I can render, let me do it now. All that I own has been given to me by the man above, and now, I must give back. I find this time in my life filled with a range of emotions. And, if I were to write my life's legacy, I would offer the following themes:

First: Dream big, my Darlings! Never settle for average. You are given but one shot at life, make the most of it. You never know how high you can climb until you are called to rise.

Second: Continue to learn. Read more books and watch less TV. Learning is a habit that will broaden your horizons and prepare you to win. And, by all means, use common sense.

Third: Appreciate all that you've been given, no matter how much or how little. Learn how to create, value, and manage your wealth. That means knowing how to apply God's principles of abundance. Never be so focused on escaping poverty that you become lost in the land of working and spending.

Fourth: Share your heart as well as your wealth. Love, the most priceless of gifts, rests within your heart. The best relationships are those where the love for each other is greater than the need for each other. Never allow the tests of life to paralyze your ability to love. When you say, "I'm sorry," look the person in the eye. When you say, "I love you," mean it. Each of us has been instructed: Whatsoever we give will be given back, in good measure, pressed down, shaken together, and running over.

Fifth: Learn from your mistakes and keep pushing. We all remember moments when something inside asked, "You did what?" "You've got to be kidding?" "How could you?" Well, I'm here to tell you to relax. Whatever happens, happens. When moments like these occur, start over; give it another try. When you do, you pay yourself the highest honor: faith and trust.

And sixth: Seek to be more Christ-like, according to His excellence. This final lesson I was forced to learn the hard way.

After your father and I parted ways, I raised you as a single parent. It wasn't easy. As if being sole provider isn't tough enough, society casts a negative shadow with the title and I was resentful. It was no secret, I helped to fuel that negativity by leaving bitter imprints on your heart regarding your father. I tried my best to get you to close off your world to him, and for that, I deeply apologize. When God made me look into the mirror of self examination I didn't like what I saw. You and I shared both prayers and tears and, with Spirit nudging me along the way, I repented for allowing my hurt and anguish to influence your thinking. I am grateful that you two are repairing your relationship. Not only do I ask for your forgiveness, but I have sought your father's as well.

As a grandmother in her fifties, I have learned many lessons, the majority of which I have yet to master. But this I know to be true: We will not be here forever. The Bible says, "It is appointed unto man once to die, and after death, judgment." It is the in between that is worthy of our attention.

With love and great anticipation,
Linda Howard McKinnie

✦　　✦　　✦

April 28, 1999
Brooklyn, NY

IF I COULD LIVE MY LIFE AGAIN

I never knew my mother, she died when I was quite young. I was raised by an aunt, and to her, I am grateful beyond words. She shaped my life. She had an answer for any slight or injustice that my self-image may have suffered during the day. She would place me before a mirror, give me an incredulous look backed up by these strong words: "Look at yourself. You are black and you are beautiful. Look at your skin. It is so smooth and soft, and dark. You can wear any color in the rainbow. There's something about you that no one can take from you." My aunt knew that real self-esteem begins with your ability to define the world on your own terms.

My aunt's efforts to instill self-esteem in me were successful, but there were many lessons I did not learn until much later in life. So, if I could live my life again, I wouldn't let anything worry me. So what if the light bill doesn't get paid on time. What's all the fuss? No sense getting your blood pressure up. If I could live my life again I would do whatever I darn well please. After all, it's a free country. I would step out on faith and wouldn't worry about making mistakes. If I could live my life again I wouldn't waste my time dipping my big toe into the water waiting for life to feel just right. I would jump right in! I would have more fun. I would learn something new every day. I would do a little bit more. I would respect other people and try to understand them a little bit more. I would hug a little bit more. I would laugh a little bit more. I would take time to smell the roses. If I could live my life again I would always put fresh flowers on the table. I would use the good China more often. I would read my Bible and I would not be so quick to judge those who didn't read it at all. I would encourage others to love their fellow man. I would bake more cakes and cookies, and I wouldn't care who licked the spoon.

This is my gift of love,
Fannie Dickerson

♦   ♦   ♦

March 7, 2000
Tulsa, OK

DO IT NOW!

If I could offer one bit of advice to my grandchildren it would be to commit the following poem to memory. Though the author is unknown, these words have made a positive influence on my life:

So, if you've got a job to do, do it now
If it is one you wish you were through, do it now.
If you are sure the job is your own,
Do not hem and haw or groan. Do it now.
Do not put off a bit of work,
It does not pay to shirk.
If you want to fill a place and be useful to the race,
Just get up and take a brace, do it now.
Do not linger by the way,
You will lose if you delay. Do it now!

Calevea McQuarters

❖   ❖   ❖

CLOSING COMMENTS ON LIVE THIS DAY

October 19, 2000
Hopewell, VA

Don't wait for someone else to say that you're a success—tell yourself! At some point in your life you must make a decision: You can focus on what you can do or what you can't. It is so easy to make excuses. You can decide to make things happen; watch things happen; or wonder what in the world happened. Every creation on God's green earth has a purpose. The purpose of life is not to be happy, but to matter. Never back away from your dreams. If your head and heart are urging you to pursue your goals, step up and meet the challenge. Judge success by what you've sacrificed, not by what you've attained.

Martha Rodgers-James

September 14, 1998
Gadsden, AL

Life is not to be taken lightly. It is a gift from God that is too valuable to be wasted. We cannot choose how or when we will die. We can only choose the manner in which we will live.

Nerva L. Daniel

❖   ❖   ❖

June 17, 1999
Chattanooga, TN

One today is worth a handful of tomorrows.

Elizabeth Jones

❖   ❖   ❖

October 1997
Hampton, VA

There are at most a few things worth dying for. Find out what yours are, and you will really be able to live.

Korine Hudson

December 28, 1999
Decatur, GA

Seize the moment with gladness. Walk in the sunshine and live with vitality. Tomorrow is not promised, nor is today. Celebrate each day by living in the moment. Living in the moment means releasing the past and not waiting for the future. Believe in your heart and stand on your beliefs. Reach within when all without is chaotic. Hate no one, for hatred breeds sickness. Love always, for love enlarges life. Today is yours to savor.

Deborah Lestage

Chapter Three

Hope

*S*ooner or later nearly everyone comes to a place in life when going on seems futile—when we are overwhelmed by the events of the day, when there seems to be nothing solid on which to stand. Perhaps your day has been filled with failure and disappointment. Perhaps you've been battered by tragedy, swallowed up by pain, and hemmed in by setbacks. Maybe you're sick, lonely, battling addictions, frustrated, fighting low self-esteem, and are adrift in life. If you are blessed to live a long life, you will surely witness personal triumphs and face a host of challenges. You will experience good times as well as bad, and no one can escape the bad. You will laugh heartily, and you will wail in pain. These are the realities that face us all. Simply stated, such is life.

According to these real-life heroines there have been times in their lives when they've approached seemingly insurmountable hurdles, times when it seemed as if all were lost. And yet, just at the right moment, at their lowest point, something beyond their control quelled the storm, straightened out the tangle, renewed their spirits, and blew away the clouds. In the words of one eighty-year-old matriarch, "I don't know where and I don't know when, but I do know a change is going to come—if you hold on."

Hope. It is a marvelous emotion that bolsters the soul. Suddenly your load is lifted, your spirit is refreshed, and your eyes regain their sparkle. Something has changed. Winds shift, tides turn, and barriers are withdrawn. Hope tones up the body and invites you to press on. Hope is the secret weapon of the soul that allows us to persevere even when the facts seem damning and the truth unbearable. Hope can turn back the hands of time, renew the spirit of youth, and make dreams come true. Hope has been known to open the door to love and friendship. It is the Moses that has led the human race out of the wilderness and promises to handle whatever comes along. If you put your heart into it, hope will provide you with success in whatever you do. Its power is limitless, and its value far surpasses money and influence. Hope makes men, men, and women, women. Single-handedly, the man or woman armed with its magic will dominate and win the day. There is no person, no position, no challenge that cannot be affected by its force. Hope tramples over prejudice, spurns indifference, and overwhelms all obstacles. The optimistic will embrace it and the vain will overlook it. Without hope in the future, there's no joy in the present. Hope is the quality that breeds faith, self-control, strength of will, cheerfulness, and a handful of other life-changing virtues which the hopeless will never know. Without it nothing can be accomplished. It is really the secret to achievement.

As you read the letters in this chapter, you will discover how these wise grandmothers have found and utilized the power of hope—solid, stable, earthshaking hope. Hope to press on. Hope to endure. Hope to stay true to the mark. Hope, the language of the heart, is the golden gem these sages hold in abundance. Hope. It's what got them over. Hope. It's what they've tried to instill in their children and are determined to pass on to you. All the darkness and despair cannot snuff out the light of one single candle. Where hope lives, hope thrives. Today so many people feel helpless, overwhelmed by the stress of everyday life. They can't convince themselves that they can make a difference, and consequently, they don't even try. They bury their talents and allow their spirits to wither on the vine of life. Poverty, crime, and good relationships gone bad confront them day after day, until hopelessness becomes a way of life. When they reach this point, few realize that they have lost faith in God's ability to assist them. How sad. Despite our ocean of tears, we must never forget that we still possess the potential and power to change our lives. You and I have the ability to improve our circumstances because God has never placed anyone in a hole from which he or she cannot climb. All too often, what some may term good luck is nothing more than the good Lord. Our Creator never closes one door without opening another. So wipe away your tears. Never doubt again. The man above is not a halfway God. If you are locked in a prison of pity, remember, you hold the key not only to your imprisonment, but to your freedom as well. Every day, in some small way, light your little candle to a life of possibilities.

September 6, 2000
Waipahu, HI

A PLACE CALLED HOPE (I)

There's a point where Heaven and earth meet. It's a place called hope. No life is without problems. I know—I've had my share. I've had to climb to every place worth reaching. Sometimes hope seems in short supply but keep looking up. Believe in life with a large YES and a small no.

Ophelia Green

❖   ❖   ❖

February 6, 2000
Baltimore, MD

THE POWER OF HOPE

I've been blessed with a six-year-old grandson, a nine-year-old grand-daughter, and the potential for more grandchildren to come. If I could leave but one piece of advice it would be simply this:

Life offers few guarantees. Bank on it. There will be times when you will be stuck or stalled. You will be burdened with difficulties suggesting that life is unfair. Sometimes it rains and it seems as if the tears will never stop falling. Personally, I don't think life is unfair, but it can be trying. We've all got dues to pay; however, it's the challenges that force us to turn inward. Without our burdens we would never know the power of hope.

You were placed in this world with a sacred obligation to use your God-given talents and abilities to the do the best you can, for as long as you can. There's little room in this world for a life without hope. Don't take my word for it. Go ask the struggling student; sit down with the cancer patient; walk the streets with the unemployed; bounce from job to job with the alcoholic; watch the single parent who pours every ounce of her being into her home and children. Those who overcome can always look to unwavering hope as the key that unlocked the door to their survival. Your finest hour will grow out of your greatest burden. If you can look to the past and smile, you still have hope. If you can find beauty in this world, you still have hope. If you can find the good in others, you still have hope. If you believe yourself worthy of what this world has to offer, you still have hope. Accept yourself, gratefully. Value yourself, confidently. Trust yourself, prayerfully, and empower yourself, wholeheartedly. Hold your head high and march on.

This may be the day you cry but it isn't the day you quit!
Laurie Drummond

❖ ❖ ❖

December 19, 2000
Decatur, GA

THE HOPE AND CONTRIBUTIONS OF
GENERATIONS GONE BEFORE

To my arrows shot into the future,

One of the most trying tasks in life is to hold words in your heart waiting for the right moment to speak them. Nothing is more powerful than timely ideas bound with deep passion. As your mother and grandmother, I want to leave you with what, I know, will serve as a reminder that we are one people with a common history and a shared destiny. May my words be of encouragement. May you share them with your children as I have so freely shared with you.

I was ten years old when me and my baby brother accompanied our mother on a bus ride from the projects of New York City to Washington, D.C. There, on the steps of the Lincoln Memorial, we sat and listened to the stirring words of a young preacher—Martin Luther King, Jr.—speak on behalf of millions whose voices had never been heard. For the sake of her children, my mother felt compelled to be a part of the civil rights movement. She wanted us to know that we could do anything or become anybody. Our only requirement would be to put forth the faith and effort to reach our dreams.

My mother was born in Savannah, Georgia. By her teenage years she had traveled north in search of better opportunities. There, Mother would graduate from high school, move to Harlem and immediately begin work as a nurse's aide. Soon, she and my father would marry only to separate ten years later. Always the fitting example, Mother went back to school, sharpened her secretarial skills, and worked for the City Hospital of New York for nearly thirty years. Upon retirement she packed up and moved back to Georgia where, for the first time in her life, she bought her own home. Imagine, she lived and raised her two small children in that New York City housing project for forty years! Mother wasn't the best or most educated, but the ideas she shared on life allowed me to find many an open door. She was the one who worked hand over fist to send me to college. In my book, there's no one better.

To this day, I can still see her face staring out the window as our bus arrived in the nation's capital. She was so excited about the trip that she didn't sleep for days. Think about it. The efforts of so few would eventually allow so many—my mother included—to vote for the first time. As for me, I guess you could say I was like a child on Christmas morning. So many black people from different parts of the country, all coming together with a deep sense of community and sharing a common purpose: To make Dr. King's dream reality. Whether sharing picnic baskets or box lunches, everyone acted like family. Nearly a decade had passed before I fully understood my mother's words. "Election day," she said, "is the only day we are all equal. The rich, the poor, white and black, each of us can vote for whomever we believe in. At one time this act was a privilege for some, but now it is a right for all."

My mother's words have gone a long way to shape my soul. But no one could have anticipated how her commitment to the struggle on this hot, steamy, historic day, as well as the hope and contributions of generations gone before, would do more to lift burdens, erase barriers, and ensure the steps of your generation as you walk this long and difficult road. May you never forget.

I pray I, too, have been a worthy example,
Denise Gines

❖   ❖   ❖

September 9, 1997
Palmdale, CA

HOPE—IT'S WHAT KEEPS ME STANDING!

I had hope that one day my children would benefit from a life full of promise. I instilled in them the fear of God, which is the beginning of wisdom. All came to know Him for themselves. Hope is all that we have. Hope rewards the faithful, provides confidence to the timid, and showers the down-and-out with self-respect and affection. Hope makes the muscles strong, the complexion rosy, and the rest doubly sweet. Hope never runs scared. Hope is the secret weapon of the soul that allows us to persevere when the facts seem troubling and the truth unbearable. Hope moves potential into power. Hope—it's what keeps me standing! Hope for a better tomorrow, hope for our children to turn out okay. Hope for the chance to make their dreams come true. Hope that they will give back to their communities and lift the race higher. Hope puts a smile on our face when the heart cannot manage. Hope places our feet on the path when our eyes cannot see. Hope moves us to act when our souls are confused about the direction.

> When we give the gift of hope, we are giving a timeless treasure,
> Johnnie Mae Johnson

◈　　◈　　◈

April 28, 1999
Harlem, NY

THE POSITIVE EXPECTATION OF A BRIGHT TOMORROW

Life is packed full of obstacles. Sometimes when you overcome one, another is lurking nearby. After twenty-five years as a legal secretary, I was forced to quit because I am a diabetic and the disease has slowly robbed me of my sight. At the time, I didn't know what to do. After all, this was my dream job. I loved the work and the pay was good. But my eyes began to fail me. Discouragement, however, is a part of living. You learn to take the bitter with the sweet. Sometimes in life there are no perfect endings. Some poems don't rhyme, some stories don't make sense, and some things just don't work out. But God is good, and I made do. Hope is knowing that you will make it through. Hope is believing in abundance while staring poverty in the face. Hope is understanding that miracles can open up your life in ways you've never imagined. Hope is surrendering your dreams and burdens to a power greater than yourself. Need I say more? Yes, hope! As the good book teaches: "We glory in tribulations knowing that trials produce perseverance; and perseverance, character; and character, hope" [Romans 5:3]. And hope does not disappoint. There's no cure like hope, no treatment so great, and no remedy so powerful as the positive expectation of a bright tomorrow.

The Lord has placed a hinge on your knees. It would be nice to thank Him every morning for the hope of a new day.

Frances Diaz

❖　　❖　　❖

May 25, 1997
Oceanside, CA

OVERCOMING OBSTACLES

My grandson graduated first in his class from Grambling State University with a 3.98 grade point average. Through all the tears of joy and happiness on that day, I felt a twinge of sadness, as his father failed us again. He did not attend his son's college graduation. But nothing would keep me from celebrating this day, a day I had waited for my entire life. My grandson's graduation represents a flame of hope to me and, even though it meant that I had to travel by bus from southern California to Grambling, Louisiana, to watch that boy with these tired old eyes march across the stage to receive his degree, it was a burden I was more than willing to bear.

I've chosen to write to you regarding a subject in which I am well versed. Twenty plus hours by bus can be a humbling experience, but Lord, what an excellent opportunity to minister to others. The following story was told to me by my mother who left to be with our Lord at age ninety-seven. Read it again and again. I believe it holds a special message.

A farmer had an old mule who was frail and deaf. After a visit from the vet the farmer was told there was nothing he could do for the poor animal but to put it out of its misery. After much discussion with his family, the farmer couldn't bear to shoot the sickly beast, so he and his wife devised a plan. They dug a huge hole near a creek on their farm, had the mule lowered down, and began shoveling dirt over the animal's weakened body. However, as dirt rained down from above, instinctively, the mule removed each scoop by stomping, packing, and shaking its back, filling the hole in the process. The more dirt they shoveled, the more the mule shaked and stomped, rising up higher and higher. By the time the farmer had pitched the last shovel, this once weak, tired old mule, with the attitude of fortitude, with true grit and determination to burn, kicked, stomped, and stood tall before fleeing to freedom. Why? Because its hoofs were on solid ground. What appeared as if it would bury him, actually blessed him—all because of the manner in which the animal handled its adversity.

So whenever you find yourself in a hole with no way out; whenever life begins to throw dirt on you and your dreams—stop digging, stop crying. Just shake off those negative feelings and use them as stepping stones to reach your higher calling.

> You are my hope,
> Gloria Cosgrove-Greene

◆   ◆   ◆

January 4, 1999
Hampton, VA

WHERE THERE IS HOPE, THERE'S LIFE

At some point in life you will be faced with a crisis that seems so overwhelming, it will shake you to the core. A loved one dies, a marriage crumbles, disease strikes, a child goes astray, or life savings are squandered. But this I know. Into each life a little rain is going to fall.

In June 1992, I was diagnosed with cancer. Following surgery I faced months of chemotherapy. Each treatment lasted four hours and left me so weak I needed assistance just to function. I lost my appetite as well as weight, and my hair came out in clumps. Being bald was the least of my worries. I had to learn to inject myself as part of the treatment to keep my white blood cell count up. To be honest, I didn't know if I was going to make it.

When you come nose to nose with the Grim Reaper, your entire outlook changes. Cancer is a harsh teacher. Suddenly you realize that as long as you're running from death, you're not really living. You realize you won't be here forever, and what follows is a fierce determination to squeeze every drop of juice from the moments you have left. I had nearly given up hope. But, at my hour of need, the Lord spoke to me as He so often does, and I thought: This is not the end. What can cancer do? Cancer cannot control my outlook. Cancer cannot steal my faith. It cannot destroy my peace. It cannot erase my memories. It cannot invade my spirit, and it will not shatter my hope. Where there is hope, there is life, and I choose to live!

I thank God to be able to wake up each morning and move under my own power. But, if I didn't, I'm confident I could handle it. There's still hope—if not for me, then for someone else. I would instruct my doctors to give my eyes to the boy who cannot see; to give my ears to the little girl who cannot hear; to give my heart to the woman who has known nothing but pain; and to give my kidneys to the child chained to dialysis. Regardless of your circumstances, you have so much to hope for.

Be ye steadfast, unmovable, unshakeable, and guided by His word,
Marie Burnett

June 5, 2001
Douglasville, GA

HE'S AN ON-TIME GOD, YES HE IS

How will I be known? A few years ago I asked my oldest son that exact question. After a moment of soul searching he replied, "Mother, you've always been a good parent. We may not have had all we wanted to eat, but at least we ate. You've been our anchor, our hope. You're the one individual who managed to keep us all together, and we are eternally grateful." My son's words caused me to pause.

I am a mother of thirteen who married at age sixteen. With ten children in tow, my husband walked out. Isn't it funny? He claimed our best interest at heart. He said he felt a calling from the Lord and was guilt ridden about the economic hardship such a career move would impose. "I'll just leave," he said. "That way you and the children won't be forced to do without." And with that, he left. I only heard from him when he was faced with the proposition of paying child support or going to jail. Other than that, he never sent a dime. I've never been one to brood, but when will our men understand how much a family can mean? The last I heard he was living in Florida with another woman. So much for his spiritual quest.

Now, thankfully, my children are grown, and, I might add, all are doing well. Lord knows, it hasn't been easy. Some folks are born with silver spoons in their mouths. I was given a strong back because I would need it. For nearly seventy years I carried a burden that went beyond the routine. It's one thing to witness the type of poverty I've seen, but it's altogether different when you've got a ringside seat. I've had hard times to burn. I grew up dirt poor in Macon, Georgia. My mother was a domestic and my father worked in a box factory before dying way before his time. Me and my four brothers and sisters shared a bedroom and a bed—bathroom in the backyard, no hot or cold running water. I bore the brunt of many schoolyard jokes. I tried to take my classmates' barbs in stride, but sometimes children can be so cruel, saying nasty things such as "You're nothing." "You're nobody." "You'll never amount to much." They can say what they want, but I was the only one in my family and neighborhood who finished high school.

After my marriage fell apart I was forced to take center stage. I worked as a practical nurse during the day and cleaned homes at night. I walked and ran from one job to the next because food and shelter for my family came before bus fare. But I'm no charity case. Through it all, neither I nor my children ever spent a day on welfare. It took a little bit more effort for me to make it. Many times when I made my rounds at the hospital, without my supervisor or coworkers' knowledge, I would wrap up leftovers taken from the trays of patients in order to feed my children. A pat of butter here, a slice of bread there. Now, don't get me wrong, I've got pride. But there are times when you've got to bite your bottom lip and move on. I can recall the countless nights on my knees begging the man above to show me a way in which I could keep my house or pay the light bill or buy gifts for Christmas. There were times when the money came late, and times when it didn't come at all—but somehow, someway, the Lord allowed me to see my way clear. He is an on-time God, yes He is.

I try not to think of the past but when I do, I know I've been blessed. In spite of a recent stroke—six weeks chained to a hospital bed and a walker was long enough for me—I can honestly say that life is much better. My struggles have not only strengthened me but have solidified my family as well. I live with a daughter who, like her brothers and sisters, is doing rather well. Most of my children are college grads and my oldest son retired from the Army as a Lieutenant Colonel—only a hop, skip, and a jump away from becoming a general.

As I've told my grandchildren, life doesn't always play fair, and you can't worry about what you can't control. On your journey you'll encounter problems that must be solved, hurdles that must be cleared, and milestones to cross. Life has a way of building barriers that you cannot climb over or tunnel underneath. Sometimes you've got to step out of the way and wait until your walls just collapse. When I look at my life, with its ups and downs and sideways steps, one thing holds true: Hope. Yes, there were moments when my palms got sweaty, times when I lost my will to fight and I braced myself for the worst. But I never gave up hope! I've tried to move forward as best as I could with what I had been given. You, too, should do no less. So calm yourself, shrug it off, steady your course, don't dwell on the past or fret about the future. Just lift your head up and keep your back straight and run the race that is set before you. No matter what sorrow and heavy sigh life has brought before you, don't stop until you see morning. Weeping may endure for a night, but joy cometh in the morning. This too shall pass. Some things you are not meant to change, but to survive. So if you cannot alter it, then outlive it. Morning does come; it lies at the end of every night. It's at the end of all limitation. It's at the end of every divorce and broken home. It's at the end of every heartache and hardship; every setback, calamity, and affliction. But when it's over, morning does come. Surely, the same power that created the heavens is strong enough to sustain you. If you will do your part, I promise you, the Lord will do His.

I've prayed many prayers when no answer came, though I've waited patient and long; but answers have come to enough of my prayers to make me keep praying on.

Without hope there is no place to go . . .

Elizabeth Pitts

June 20, 2001
Toledo, OH

WHAT THE DYING TEACH US

I wrote this letter twice. Once in my mind, another with my arthritic hand. Each time the result was the same. My child is lying in the next room fighting for her life. Of my three children, Sharon is my only daughter. If there is a chart that measures grief, then losing a child must rank at the top. I know it's tough losing a spouse, a sibling or, for that matter, any loved one. But saying good-bye to someone who you gave life to is a loss you survive but never get over. I can't imagine life without her, but now *I am forced to*.

My daughter was both beautiful and talented. Always a good student, she studied business in college and loved to sing and dance. Not all children grow up to be a Beethoven or a Mozart, but Sharon definitely has a gift for music. At her grandmother's funeral she sang "Safe in His Arms" like she wrote it. And to be such a little thing, Lord could she eat! She loved collard greens and hot water cornbread. A few years ago at our family reunion in Detroit, Sharon was so energetic and vibrant. She had so much energy. Full of dreams and goals, she was a picture of health. She firmly believed that she owed the world a living, not vice versa. Now she may never get the chance, and the world will be much poorer for it.

Sharon had just turned fifty when she complained of severe stomach pain. After months of declining health a team of doctors ran a battery of tests. It didn't take long. At Atlanta's Crawford Long Hospital she was diagnosed with advanced ovarian cancer. A tumor the size of a brick and just as hard, was found near her intestine. When given the results she was in denial and I, her mother, was devastated. A few years back I had lost my mother to the same disease. I just couldn't deal with it. I've always considered myself lucky and optimistic, but a diagnosis of cancer is the one piece of news that can shake your confidence in a happy ending.

When I received the phone call, before my daughter even mentioned the word, I could hear it in her voice.

Almost immediately Sharon endured chemotherapy and radiation treatment. As expected, she lost her long, beautiful hair, not to mention her desire to eat. But somehow she refused all sympathy. "I'll be alright," she would tell us. "Just wait and see." Her spirit seemed to know that ovarian cancer may be the diagnosis but a lack of hope will decide the final outcome. All that pain and optimism found its reward when her cancer went into remission. For a few months Sharon began to rally. Little by little, she regained her strength as well as her appetite. Momentarily, we won the battle; we snatched her back from death's door. But in the long run the disease would flare up again. Cancer would not be an easy foe. Less than five weeks ago she took a turn for the worse. Our doctor called us in and gave us the cold hard facts. Sharon was given less than two months to live.

Sometimes death walks with a light step; sometimes it pounds away like a hammer. Her medication is so strong it forces her to take deep breaths as her body shakes and trembles. One afternoon, I overheard her tell the nurses she was ready to go. I was too stunned to move. At fifty-eight, in the prime of her life, she is sliding toward death's door.

So here I am, by her bedside, hugging my child through tears. Watching her fight tooth and nail, and just as helpless. Seeing her lie there, she looks unreal. The plain walls in her bedroom, a virtual sanctuary, are now filled with inspiration and Bible verses. Romans 8:37 is her favorite: "We are more than conquerors." During her long illness, I pray continually. The Lord has always been there. He sat beside me during the doctor's consultations. He was there as we waited the long vigils outside the operating room. He could be found nearby when we rejoiced in the miracle of a brief recovery. He is with me now as my hope seems to be slipping away. I never kiss my daughter goodnight without wondering whether I will see her in the morning. When I arise I greet each new day as though she were newly born, a fresh chance at life. Now, every moment that I have been given with my daughter is a moment of grace and hope.

I guess when you look at the big picture, we're all on borrowed time. By the time it takes to read my letter each of us could be face-to-face with our Maker. We could all be gone with the blink of an eye. Now, I am not trying to scare you or pressure you. I am simply trying to help you see clearly. As my daughter has confronted her demons, she has taught us so much. Ask her doctors and nurses who would give and do anything to heal her body. Ask her family and friends who are inspired by her courageous example. Ask her pastor who, time and time again, found my daughter in her hour of anguish praising His holy name. And ask me, her mother, who can recall the days I held this child close to my bosom, how simple life can be. Never give up hope.

> *If I knew this would be the last time that I'd see you fall asleep*
> *I would tuck you in tightly and pray the Lord, your soul to keep,*
> *If I knew this would be last time that I'd see you walk out the door*
> *I'd hug and kiss you and call you back for more;*
> *If I knew this would be the last time that I could spare a moment or two,*
> *I'd say I Love You instead of assuming that you know I do.*

Done made my vow and I'm never turning back,
Gladys Russell

❖   ❖   ❖

January 9, 2001
Houston, TX

A PLACE CALLED HOPE (2)

Their names are Tarin and Dameon. Fourteen years ago, they were my youngest great-grands that I was forced to meet under trying circumstances. Tarin, the oldest, was barely two years old, and Dameon, his little brother, was about to turn one. In spite of the manner in which we met, they were so sweet and innocent. Still are. Handsome, they look like their mother—my granddaughter. Two cute little things who would snuggle nicely under my chin. They were good eaters and good sleepers, too. As soon as I got home from work I would rock them all evening. Most of the time they slept, but while they were awake, I read, sang, and stroked their heads. They listened attentively and smiled big, beaming smiles. They seemed to recognize their Granny and know how much I loved them.

I want Tarin and Dameon to be happy. Common sense tells me they'll have some problems and rough spots along the way. So I say a prayer for them—that when they cannot be safe, they'll be brave. On the surface they appear to be loved and quite adapted. But I know better.

Most of the time I see them as a mystery. I know I'm not responsible for them, then again, I am. The boys' mother has been in and out of jail and doesn't show the slightest sign of interest. Their grandparents are equally as indifferent. They don't want them, either. And their father? Well, don't get me started. He washed his hands of the whole mess a long time ago. The courts don't even know what to do. I worry about this chaotic world they are entering. It seems more out of touch than at anytime I can remember. That's the only conclusion I can come up with. I mean, how in the name of everything decent could this woman, my granddaughter and their mother, do what they did?

The first time I saw my boys they were standing in the middle of the room in a trailer house with their arms fully extended. They seemed to be saying, "Granny, take me!" It's been said that the Lord takes care of fools and babies. I guess their mother knew that proverb all too well. This could be the only reason why she would leave her babies in the middle of nowhere in the dead of the night. It was one-thirty in the morning when I received the phone call. To make a long story short, she and the boys' father—"some long, tall black man," she would later tell a judge— were high on crack. A fight ensued and after all the yelling and cussing a neighbor awoke to discover that the two toddlers had been dumped on her doorstep.

"Ms. Joyce," the woman explained, "I'm sorry to disturb you, but this is Miss Such-and-Such, and you won't believe what happened." All that I can remember of that phone call were the words "they'll be here whenever you're ready." And with that, I jumped out of bed, threw on some clothes, and drove more than three hundred miles—from Houston, Texas, to Minden, Louisiana—to pick the children up.

Because of their mother's drug habit there's no telling where these babies have been. I just thank God that dear woman called, and that I could be reached. She had seen my granddaughter on a number of occasions, undoubtedly in a drugged-out daze, and the two spoke ever so briefly. In the course of those conversations I guess she spoke of me, her great-grandmother who lives in Houston. When I pulled into her driveway the sun wasn't even up. The children were still in their pajamas, and, as you can imagine, a bit groggy. Before leaving, this dear woman pieced together the complete story. Shocked senseless, I shook my head, hugged her, and cried. As a matter of fact, we both cried. Raising children alone is difficult enough, but when you're sixty years old and diagnosed with a brain tumor, this could be your final act on the stage of life.

I know all about Minden, Louisiana. I was born and raised in a three-room broken-down shack on a dirt road nearby, about thirty miles outside of Shreveport. Nothing in this part of Louisiana has changed. Whites still live on one side of the tracks and colored on the other. Like everyone else in this corner of the state, we were farmers. We picked peas, corn, and cotton from dusk to dawn. And, like everybody else, our life was consumed by trying to figure out how to survive with more days in the month than money in the bank. My parents could neither read nor write. I was the third of seven children, three boys and four girls. None of us had a bed to ourselves. Usually we'd sleep three to a bed, two in the middle and one up against the railing. Sometimes my brothers or sisters would even sleep on the floor. In the winter my father had to chop plenty of firewood for our stove, otherwise we'd freeze. We were too poor for indoor plumbing. Come to think of it, I didn't know anyone who had running water. We had an outhouse, tar paper roof with a concrete floor. Everything we ate came off our farm and many times that wouldn't be enough. There were many a day when breakfast consisted of grits and butter.

We lived so far out in the sticks that the walk to and from school was nearly twenty miles. As soon as I got home I washed the one dress I had to my name to be sure I had something clean to wear in the morning. I quit school in the eighth grade and worked as a domestic. So many of my friends did the same thing. I wasn't any different. As I look back, I guess that's why I ran out of my house when I received the phone call that changed my life. I didn't want anyone—particularly my grandchildren—to experience what I've been through.

Three years would pass before we heard from my granddaughter again. There seemed to be a million rumors as to her whereabouts, but not even a hint of her existence. Then one day, without warning, she appeared at my door wearing an orange prison jump suit holding two little infants—and I mean infants! The youngest, not even two weeks old, had neither a name or a birth certificate. What happened to her clothes, I'll never know. But a better question would've been, "What happened to her pride?" She had spent a year in jail for breaking and entering. During her time away she had also been in and out of treatment centers and detox units in Homestead, Florida, while on the run from the law. By her twenty-first birthday, she had a lengthy rap sheet. One night she confided that she had hit bottom a thousand times. She told me that each time she smokes crack she promises herself that it will be the last time. I wish I could believe her. I know that her addiction is really a disease, but I've decided long ago nothing will come before her children. Neither I, nor her boys, and now her two little girls, will be treated like doormats. I've worked two jobs for the longest, trying to keep food on the table and a roof over our heads. As the years go by I can feel my health slipping away, and I am definitely not in the mood for broken promises. My granddaughter has no job, no schooling, no goals, no sense of direction, and no peace. And now, she has four children, each conceived in a fog of drugs and alcohol, I pray she gets her life together. I'm probably the only person standing between these children and the foster care system.

Initially, I agreed to keep the girls—only a year apart—for just a few weeks. Call me a soft touch. But I've also decided to end their personal nightmare. Shortly after the girls arrived, they would follow me from room to room as if I was about to leave them. Even at an early age they can sense when they're unwanted. No matter how much you love them, a child never gets over the feeling of being abandoned. When I set the paperwork in motion to adopt, I had little trouble receiving complete custody. My granddaughter, whether in rehab, paroled, or on the run, kept making tearful phone calls to her court-appointed lawyer in Houston. However, impatient when a new relapse landed her back in jail, the Department of Human Services and Family Court terminated her parental rights.

Now that all four of my great-grandchildren have been given a fresh chance at life, they seem to be making the most of it. They are rooted. They know they have a place to call home. All are excellent students. All share their love openly and none of them have ever given me an ounce of trouble. They're just like me—they don't demand much. If you could've seen what they gave me last Mother's Day, you would've sunk to your knees. Who came up with the idea is not important. But for weeks they saved and pooled their lunch money until they had enough to buy me flowers, earrings, and the sweetest card. I cried all morning. The two boys, ages fifteen and fourteen, are quite serious. One wants to be an engineer, and the other, inspired by Colin Powell, hopes to make the military his career. As for those precious girls—they're eleven and ten. They both love science and medicine. Who knows where their dreams will lead. I've told each child they have a specific challenge as well as a specific calling. I just pray I'm around to see them come true. As of this writing, they have no idea how sick I've been. Oh, they know that sometimes

Granny doesn't feel well, and that she's been in and out of the hospital. But they don't know the particulars of the cancer or the extent. And there's no need for them to know. They only need to know that I will always be here for them.

It shouldn't be hard to be a child. Children should live in a world where life is much simpler, and not as rushed. A world where anything is possible. A world where lies, suffering, illness, and unhappy marriages don't exist. A place where everyone will live forever; where taking drugs means orange-flavored chewable aspirin. A time and place where reading is fun and music is clean. A world where everyone believes in the power of smiles, hugs, a kind word, truth and dreams. I tell my great-grandchildren there is such a place—it is a place called hope.

Here's hoping for the best,
Myrtle Joyce

❖ ❖ ❖

January 5, 1999
Hampton, VA

NOT A MOMENT WITHOUT HOPE

The Lord seeks men and women who will trust in His word. Men and women who are not afraid to take a stand; who dare to dream. Men and women who will be with God through thick and thin—not sometimey wishy-washy folks who will thin out when things get thick. You can live a lifetime without fame or fortune; weeks without food; days without water; minutes without air; but not a moment without hope! Here is the formula for spiritual success: If you want to be distressed, look within; if you want to be defeated, look back; if you want to be distracted, look around you; if you want to be dismayed, look ahead of you; but if you want to be hopeful, look up! The Lord doesn't demand that you win, but He does expect you to try. He expects you to hold on and to hold out!

Leoney Orie

❖   ❖   ❖

January 12, 1999
Hampton, VA

THIS IS YOUR MISSION

A great number of women today, especially those who are blessed to be called grandmother, will probably tell you that life holds many surprises. This is true. However, regardless of the shifting winds, never forget that God has a special plan for each of us. Our responsibility is to lean on His word as we run this race, "for in due season we shall reap if we do not lose heart" [Galatians 6:9].

As you can tell, I am a praying woman. I married the man of my dreams and raised a wonderful and loving family. At one point, life could not have been better. Then, out of the blue, challenges and heartbreak forced their way into my life. First, my son became gravely ill and was bedridden before he eventually passed away. Next, four months after the death of our son, my husband suffered a stroke that left him disabled and unable to work. And, if this were not enough, shortly after his stroke I was diagnosed with breast cancer. I was devastated.

You're probably thinking, "What's next?" I know I did. I battled each day with all my might, hoping beyond hope that my circumstances would change. Yes, there were days that I grew weary. Yes, there were times that my faith faltered. Yes, there were moments when I questioned God—"Why me? What have I done to deserve these devastating setbacks?" But I never gave up on His promise: "Life will present a slew of challenges, be strong and courageous" [Deuteronomy 31:6]. I used every ounce of my being to stay true to the mark.

Life may not always be fair, but you must never allow the pains, hurdles, and handicaps of the moment to allow you to lose hope. Your purpose in life begins with a "why," a reason to keep on keepin' on, in spite of the pain, misfortune, and heartbreak. This is your mission. Never allow anyone or any misfortune to shake your belief. You may lose your family, your friends, your health, and your fortune, but there is always hope as long as you maintain a firm faith. The Lord will remove your tears, but you've got to wipe your eyes.

I hope my story helps. Life is all about choices. You can feel sorry for yourself or you can stand on the solid rock of the Man Above and use your stumbling blocks as stepping stones. It's all up to you. The Lord will never give you more than you can bear. Hope never stands around twiddling its thumbs. Choices, not chances, will determine your future.

Annie B. Gregory

◈　　◈　　◈

June 25, 1999
Chicago, IL

YOU'VE GOT TO HAVE HOPE

When we finally lay our burdens down in the bright light of Divine truth, when we stand before the tribunal of spiritual justice, you and I will not be judged for what we've become or what we've attained. Oh, no. We will simply be asked, "Did you keep the faith? Did you lean on His every word? Did you hold on? Did you hope beyond hope?"

May this be the day when it all comes together: Happiness in your heart; serenity in your soul; success in everything you do; standing by the truth, searching for the good that is always there; going from rock bottom to mountain top; believing in tomorrow but living today; never giving up; and finding hope in hard-to-find places. If you can begin, you can continue. If you can reach out, you can hold on. And if you can hope beyond hope, you can overcome. In your hands lies the power.

THERE IS A KEY (AUTHOR UNKNOWN)

There is a key to every lock
A true desire has no stumbling block,
God has given you a wholesome mind
To trust in Him at all times.
In life, set early your goals
Record in writing that which unfolds,
Always stand on spiritual feet
For truly your still waters run deep.
When one door closes another is open
Now here is a word so fitly spoken.

Look up, Darling, you've got to have hope,
Yvette Ridley

❖　　❖　　❖

December 14, 1997
Cleveland, OH

SERVING OTHERS WHO ARE HURTING

To Iyana, Raymon, and Chenelle,

It's been said that when we are down to nothing, God is up to something. Lord knows I've been down to nothing since the day of that senseless act.

It's been eighteen years and seemingly a million sleepless nights since my daughter's body was found in the basement of an abandoned building located less than five hundred feet from her school. She was so excited about the prospect of receiving an award for perfect attendance that she left home fifteen minutes early—the longest fifteen minutes of her life. On December 6, 1984, she was abducted, raped, and murdered. How could this have happened to such an innocent child?

At the height of the investigation sixty police officers worked day and night over a two-month stretch. More than 250 neighbors, family members, teachers, and classmates were questioned. Police tightened the noose by concentrating on fifteen suspects. Any day now, the police felt, the case would be broken. But that day never came. Despite a massive manhunt, Gloria's attacker has yet to be found. Though I still wait for my baby to come running back into my life, I must and I will move on. If not for me, then for every mother who has felt this pain. Somehow, someway, you've got to plug into your purpose. Clearly, I have found my purpose: Serving others who are hurting.

Regardless of who you are or where you are, no matter if you have stumbled in the past—if you have ever hoped for a miracle that one day life would find a way to even the score, I am happy to say that your wait is over. When faced with adversity and hard times, we have a tendency to turn our backs and deny God's glory. But it's at these very times when we need hope the most. We will never experience joy until we are faced with sorrow. We will never understand faith until our limits are tested. We will never appreciate peace until we are overcome with tragedy. We will never embrace love until it is lost. And we will never experience the calming influence of hope until we are knee deep in doubt. It is hope that gives life new meaning.

Since that cold, dreary December day I've come to understand that the Man Above will either lighten our load or strengthen our back. For nearly twenty years, I've been able to bear this burden by channeling my grief into making the streets of my community safer. And I've been blessed. Several years ago former President George Bush recognized my efforts by awarding me the 908th Point of Light in his Thousand Points of Light Campaign.

So hear me well. I don't want anyone to feel sorry for me. There's a lot of light in my life. I want people to look at me and see that, in spite of the circumstances, regardless of the difficulties, they can make it. There is hope for the uneducated who believe that one day they will comprehend. There's hope for the disabled if they can imagine life beyond their affliction. And there's even hope for the hopeless—no matter how late the hour, if they will stand in the face of opposition, strengthen their grip, and cling to the faith-filled message: As long as there is life, there's hope.

Yvonne Pointer-Triplett

❖   ❖   ❖

SOME FINAL WORDS ON HOPE

October 15, 1997
Port Huron, MI

In times of sorrow and heartbreak, I've always remembered my mother's advice: "Face your disappointment, conquer it and move on." In other words, you must live by hope if you are to live at all. Faith has no time for doubt; love has no time for hate; and hope has no time for despair.

Elizabeth "Mother" Howell

December 11, 1998
Hampton, VA

Trying times are times for trying. If you don't scale the mountain you'll never see the view.

Daisy W. Alston

❖   ❖   ❖

December 1998
Hampton, VA

Life will provide its share of ups and downs. But stand tall and realize there is a stronger force behind the scenes. Every night has a new dawning; every room has a door; every lock has a key; and every problem has an answer.

Annie B. Gregory

❖   ❖   ❖

March 1, 2001
Baltimore, MD

You can't have a testimony without a test. How can you celebrate triumph unless if you've faced defeat? How can you appreciate good health until you've endured the storms of sickness? How can you appreciate the sweet taste of prosperity unless you've experienced the bitter fruit of poverty? How will you know that God is God unless your back has been pinned to the wall and your life has been saturated with pain and turmoil? The Lord is not picking on you. He's pointing you out!

Carolyn J. Young

October 1997
Port Huron, MI

The happiest people don't necessarily have the best of everything. They just make the best of everything.

Ila Shoulders

Chapter Four

Count It
All Joy!

As a child, my mother and I had our own special game that we often played in the evening before she tucked me in. We would each open her Bible at random, place our finger on whatever page faced us, and read aloud the verse we were touching. That, she always assured me, was our own special message from above to help us deal with the challenges of the day. I believed her. Though my mother is gone, last night I played our game again. As I opened my Bible, I closed my eyes and gently ran my finger down the page. When I looked, my forefinger rested on a verse from Psalm 103: "Be thankful to Him, and bless His name." And some folks say that the Lord doesn't speak to us. I gently closed my Bible, feeling more at peace.

Few of us stop to realize and appreciate the many undeserved blessings that have been heaped our way. We lament that we've been given no chance, no future, and little opportunity. No one knows or can even guess at the untold millions who are living in a heaven of opportunity and yet, turn their blessings into a living hell. They have every opportunity to love, and yet, they hate. They have every opportunity to share, and yet, they waste. They have every opportunity to work and give of themselves, and yet, they doubt their abilities and squander their talents and gifts. Sad will be the day when opportunity knocks and you fail to open the door. Opportunity pays a visit to the saint and the sinner alike. Many fail to see it, whereas the blessed few catch sight of it everywhere.

Why, the poorest soul among you has been blessed as only the Lord of heavenly hosts can bless such an individual. We, myself included, have taken so much for granted. Perhaps, now, it would be wise to ask, "What's right in my life rather than what's wrong?" What are the real positives that can be found throughout your universe? It could be your marriage of more than twenty years or the love of your children. It could be the close, endearing *friendship that have grown more meaningful with each passing day. How about your job? Say what you want but it pays the bills. And you do continue to enjoy vibrant health. I hope you realize getting old is a blessing. Some folks are gone before their time. We should be thankful for the simple, routine events of the day: a warm cup of coffee, the presence of a new friend, or an hour without pain. See if you can notice the rose in the vase rather than the dust on the table. In other words, take the time to count your blessings.*

Now, I can only guess what you're thinking. You may not buy into my idea that opportunity is more or less there for the taking or that you are blessed. You may be confused and troubled, throwing up your hands in the face of God's promises, surrendering any hope of a brighter tomorrow. Your attitude and excuses—I'm black; I'm poor; I'm female; I'm uneducated—will not find sympathy in these pages. These black grandmothers have lived through every excuse you can imagine—and then some—yet they discovered long ago that those who we call blessed are everyday souls who believe themselves to be in control of their own lives. The way they see it, you're in the right place at the right time, blessed abundantly.

For this and much more, you should be grateful. And you should express your gratitude daily—to your parents and family who've contributed to your well-being; to your friends who've given you the benefit of the doubt again and again; to your teachers and mentors who motivate, guide, and inspire you to dig deeper and to reach higher; and to your Creator from whom all blessings flow. I suggest you begin to count your blessings. Once you realize how blessed you are and how much you have going for you, the smiles will return, the clouds will fade, the sun will shine, and you will finally be able to move forward to claim the life the Almighty has planned on your behalf—with grace, dignity, and confidence.

August 1, 1997
New Orleans, LA

MY SOUL SINGS THE HYMN
"I WON'T COMPLAIN"

There seems to be a divinity that shapes our lives. Born into a family of two faiths, I was taught early in life love of a Supreme Being. My father was raised as a Catholic and my mother, Baptist. My parents were kind, compassionate, and valued education. We were poor financially, but rich in love and understanding.

After graduating from high school I attended college for one year. Oh, how I desperately wanted to teach. Though I did everything humanly possible to earn money for my tuition—from cooking and cleaning to waiting tables—a lack of funds forced me to quit. During the second world war I, like so many women my age, took a job in a factory, sewing army uniforms. There I stayed, until the conclusion of the war. I was a pretty good seamstress and the pay wasn't bad, but I never lost sight of my dream of returning to college. Twenty years later, I did just that. I earned a degree in education, and taught school until I retired. These would have been the happiest days of my life but for one exception. After thirty-four years of marriage, my husband left home, never to be heard from again. It was traumatic for me and my children.

When I begin to ponder all the could-have-beens and should-have-beens in my life, it would be so easy to second guess; so easy to be frozen with self-pity. I've drunk from the cup of disappointment and pain, and I've gone many days without a song. I've had enough trials to make me strong, and more than enough sorrow to keep me human. But my story is less about misery and more about redemption. Being single again, and forced to support a family can be tough. However, I'm thankful. Thankful the Lord continues to grant me good health. Thankful that I've been given two lovely grandchildren. And thankful that I've got a roof over my

head, I didn't question "Why me?" when the good came my way, so I'm
not going to complain when it begins to rain. I just embrace what I've
been given. I focus on my gains, not losses—my health, food, shelter,
clothing, love for others as well as their love for me.

Through His grace, I have paid off the mortgage on my home. Now
all I can say is "Thank you." My circumstances could've been worse. Yes,
my journey has been neither smooth nor easy. But am I bitter? Not
hardly. You can't look back. The brightest future will always be based on
a forgotten past.

I suggest you begin to count your blessings. Right now, just minutes
from where you sit, there are eyes that will never see; there are ears that
will never hear; hearts that have stopped beating; and minds that have
snapped beneath the weight of today's challenges. Once you realize how
blessed you are and how much you've got going for you, the smiles will
return, the clouds will fade, the sun will shine, and you will finally be able
to move forward to claim the life the Almighty has intended for you—
with grace, strength, and confidence. Take on the spirit of a grateful
heart. As you do, you give the good Lord an open door to bring about
more blessings into your life. "Behold, I have set before you an open door
which no man can shut" [Revelations 3:8] is the divine promise. The
Lord has set before each of us an open door—a wide open track to good
and grace which no unfortunate circumstance or unforeseen hardship can
block.

The Lord did not make a mistake by providing you and me with so
many gifts. In turn, our response to His grace and goodness should begin
with the words: I am blessed!

You should blow the Lord a kiss for the gift of each new day,
Jessie L. Mouton

October 6, 1997
Cleveland Heights, OH

THE ONLY TWO WORDS YOU
SHOULD EVER SPEAK

Growing up, my family was quite poor. As one of ten children, I witnessed firsthand how difficult life could be with little or no money. But at some point you've got to step back and acknowledge what's right in your world. If I had my life to live over, there's hardly anything that I would change. Though I experienced life's ups and downs, I thank God for giving me a loving husband and three wonderful children. As of this writing, we've been together for fifty-six years. There's no sense in whining about things you cannot control. Just brace yourself and continue to search for the best. Lord knows, there are enough people looking for the worst.

By counting my blessings I turn apathy into cheerfulness, despair into laughter, and grief into gratitude. When you can offer thanks in the midst of your trial, your life has taken a turn for the best. If the only two words you ever speak are "thank you," Child, you've said enough.

Eva Johnson

❖   ❖   ❖

December 11, 1998
Hampton, VA

COUNT IT ALL JOY!

Life can change in an instant. A doctor's phone call, a drunk driver's wrong turn, or a slip on a banana peel. Caught in the buzz of our daily routines, in the heat of our cell phone hustle and bustle we take so much for granted. All that really matters is a safe place in which to tuck our children into bed at night and friends who understand tough times. You get your blessing one way or another, and it need not be money.

At times it has been difficult for me to put into words the importance of counting our blessings. It's true—the sun doesn't always shine and the fruit is not always ripe. You cannot expect to walk your remaining days on earth on mountain peaks and hilltops. No matter how hard you try, there will be days, maybe even weeks and months, when all that you attempt results in frustration and failure. When these moments arrive, as they most assuredly will, follow this simple plan: If you feel depressed, sing; if you feel sad, laugh; if you feel disheartened, rejoice; and, if you feel overwhelmed, count it all joy! You're blessed when you are no longer concerned about the length of your life but only its width and depth. You're blessed when you feel you've lost what is most dear to you because only then can you be embraced by the One most dear to you. You're blessed when you understand your attitude toward life will determine life's attitude toward you. You're blessed when you can get mad, and then get over it. You're blessed if you've been given health enough to make work a pleasure; wealth enough to support your needs; strength enough to battle difficulties and overcome them; grace enough to admit your mistakes; patience enough to toil until your good is accomplished; and love enough to move you to be useful and helpful to another.

When you tally up all that you've been given, it's not what you've got in your pocket that matters. It's what you hold in your heart that counts. Today, and every day, I will count my blessings.

Geraldine B. Clark

November 30, 1998
Hampton, VA

I AM GRATEFUL

As a retired senior citizen I volunteer my time at our local hospital. I've seen a woman overtaken with asthma so bad, she had to fight for every breath. I said, "Lord, Thank you for allowing me the chance to breathe without pain." I saw a man strapped in a wheelchair who will never take another step. I praised God for the simple ability to walk.

I am grateful for those who place the welfare of others before their own personal comfort. I am grateful for those gone before who willingly planted seeds for success that you and I now harvest. I am grateful for the beauty of my extended family. Whether the skin be fair or dark, the eyes round or slanted, the hair coarse or straight, is irrelevant. We are all beautiful in His sight. Little children are beautiful. So too, are the aged, whose wrinkled hands and faces speak of struggle and survival, of the virtues and values they have embraced. But above all else, I am grateful for my belief in the Almighty and the power of prayer, the invitation to appeal to a force much greater than my own. Surely we are a blessed people, for which we ought to express gratitude and then demonstrate the depth of our appreciation by the goodness and measure of our lives. I never get over the wonder of it. How fortunate can we be?

Any day above ground is a good one,
Ellen A. Stewart

January 28, 2001
Atlanta, GA

AN ATTITUDE OF THANKSGIVING

I've always lived with an attitude of thanksgiving. Growing up poor, black, and one of eleven children, I had little choice but to be grateful for life's small blessings. I try my best to pass this outlook on to my thirty-two grandchildren and twelve great-grandchildren.

I was raised on a plantation in Warren County, Georgia. My mother and father were sharecroppers. They grew corn, beans, greens, tomatoes, and not to mention, the thickest, softest cotton this side of Augusta. I quit school after the eighth grade to work on our farm. I really had no choice. Back then, there weren't many black high schools. Black children who lived in the rural part of the state simply went to work after the eighth grade while white children continued their education. But, like the Lord does on so many occasions, He made a way. When my children and grandchildren came home from high school I would read and study their books. Still do. It wasn't the easiest thing to do but I got a chance to bolster my education.

I was barely sixteen years old when I left home to get married. My first job was that of a nanny to a wealthy family in Atlanta. Though I am black and they were white, for ten years I raised those children just like they were my own. They, in turn, treated me with all the love, courtesy, and respect one could receive. To this day, I even attend their family reunions where I am the center of attention. They continue to shower me with money and gifts. Now this is where the gratitude part comes in. Toward the end of my ten years raising these children, their father fell ill and was confined to a wheelchair. One day while I was preparing dinner, he sat motionless staring out the window looking back over his life. He rolled his chair over to me and said something that I will never forget: "Emma, people say I'm rich. Nothing could be further from the truth. I couldn't get out of this wheelchair if I tried. I can't even spend my money, no matter how much I've earned. You, on the other hand, you've got your health, your family, and your strength, and, for that, you're the richest person on earth." With those words, he pushed himself back over to the window. A man alone with his thoughts.

It's not easy being grateful all the time. But when you begin to appreciate the little blessings in life you see the world through the eyes of God. So whatever you do, be thankful. Be thankful for each new challenge, for it is an opportunity for growth and improvement. Be thankful for your mistakes, for they will teach you valuable lessons. Be thankful when you're tired and weary, for it means you've made a difference. And be thankful that your clothes fit you snug, because it means you've had enough to eat. If you find a way to be thankful for your troubles, they will become your blessings.

Emma Lowe

❖   ❖   ❖

October 8, 1997
Cleveland, OH

NOT A BURDEN, A BLESSING

Providing a loving and stable home for our children was our number one priority. I worked during the day, and my husband worked at night. When he came home his dinner was always on the table. It wasn't easy, but God made a way. Now, my children are grown and they lead productive lives. As I look back, I can see that the Lord didn't burden us with work—He blessed us with it.

Mary C. Blackmon

July 30, 2001
Charlotte, NC

PASS THE BLESSINGS ON TO OTHERS

It's your most treasured possession and it inspires each new generation. It is called opportunity. I've taught music, specifically piano, in Charlotte, North Carolina, for the past fifty years, all the while stressing to my students the need to put their talent and gifts to good use. Life can be whatever you want it to be. So many dreams are waiting to be realized providing you are willing to put your shoulder to the wheel and work to attain them. Inscribed on the walls of my studio you will find these words: "Those who want to succeed find a way; those who would rather not find an excuse."

I think the following story sums up my view on success. A young man gave a rousing performance before a large group of socialites. During the reception after the recital a woman said to the young virtuoso, "I'd give anything to play as you do."

His teacher, who had accompanied her prize pupil, overheard the woman's remark, and said with a cold stare, "Oh, no you wouldn't!"

A hush fell throughout the hall as the woman squirmed with embarrassment. In a much softer voice she repeated her original statement. "I would, too, give anything to play the piano like you."

"No you wouldn't," the teacher interrupted. "If you would, you could possibly play as well as this young man, if not better. You'd give anything to play like him except the time, discipline, and effort needed to reach such an objective. You wouldn't sit and practice, hour after hour, day after day, year after year."

Those who envy the star performers should know that men and women of accomplishment do not idly wish for success. They go after it with a vengeance. They give their dedication, their days and nights, weeks, months—years, if necessary—to pursue their dreams. God hides both ambition and opportunity in every human soul.

As a daughter of sharecroppers, I grew up barefoot in rural Franklin County—the poorest county in North Carolina—thirty miles north of Raleigh. My mother, father, and seven brothers and sisters tried to put on a happy face, but we were dirt poor. Life was reduced to finding enough money to get us through the next day. Today, my four grown children shake their collective heads when they consider the type of poverty that followed me throughout my childhood. No electricity, no refrigerator, basically, no nothing. Fortunately, whatever we lacked in money we more than made up for in love and faith.

My elementary school principal, Dr. Ellen Alston, owned a radio and, on some evenings, I would venture over to her house to sit in her dining room. There I would close my eyes and listen for hours on end. As I look back, I know her little radio didn't change my life—it probably saved it. It was through her tiny radio that I got my first taste of the great composers which was, literally, music to my ears. I listened to the music of Beethoven, W. C. Handy, and Scott Joplin. My spirit absorbed every note, from classical to rag to gospel. As a result, I dreamed of becoming a pianist. Dr. Alston sensed my desires and gave me my first piano lesson. It was her steady hand that not only taught me my first note, but exposed me to a world beyond limits. She was the master teacher who single-handedly impacted children and adults, and motivated all to achieve their dreams. She bragged endlessly about my abilities, even during those moments when I'd rather not practice. My surroundings were not a place that led anyone to think I should be reaching for such a faraway star. But with the love and support from people like Dr. Alston, they led me to believe that I could indeed complete this journey. Though everyone in our county was poor, with help from above, poverty would not be mine. For me, the door leading to a better world would be through music and education.

After the death of my father, my mother struggled to make ends meet.

We barely stayed afloat. With a hint of better opportunities to the north, my family moved to Newport News, Virginia, a stone's throw from Hampton Institute. It was here that a new course for my life would be set. One day, my sister, who worked at a drugstore, gave me a tour of the campus. I was in awe. I walked through the buildings, saw the library, met teachers and students, and soaked in Hampton's rich cultural history. Everything and everybody appeared so distinguished and polished, with the highest degree of decorum. To put it mildly, Hampton lit my flame and my future was clear: Somehow, someway, I was going to attend this fine institution and study music. My spirit would accept nothing less. For the next few years, I devoted myself completely to my academics. If I wasn't practicing piano, I was either saving money or trying to hunt down a scholarship. And then, in 1948, thanks to family, friends, and, of course, the Divine hand, it all came together. I graduated cum laude from Hampton Institute before eventually moving on to receive my master's degree.

Since the day I earned my degree, I've felt that I've been charged with certain duties and responsibilities: to pry open closed minds, to enable others to seize opportunities, and to point out to our younger generation all of the spellbinding possibilities. In short, to be a blessing. For the past fifty years, through music and education, I have sought to enrich and arouse the lives of our children. As a teacher, it is personally rewarding when a former pupil acknowledges your efforts. Such was the case of Daniel Anthony Heath, a fine young man and one of my best students. Though his family is of modest means, Daniel set his sights on attending Morehouse College in Atlanta, Georgia. I will never forget the day his mother, incredulous at the thought, approached me and said, "Mrs. Jones, I cannot afford to send my son to Morehouse."

To which I replied, "You cannot afford not to!" And with that, I began the process of raising money for his tuition.

Between financial aid, grants and scholarships, and, to be on the safe side, the $1,000 that my husband and I kicked in, I am happy to say that Daniel is a 4.0 music/pre-law major at Morehouse College. He hopes to become an entertainment lawyer. As a way of thanking me for what I had done, Daniel sent the following letter of endorsement to the North Carolina Arts and Science Council on my behalf. It reads, in part:

> It is indeed my pleasure to endorse Mrs. Clara Jones as a candidate for your assessment. Mrs. Jones has given her time, wisdom, money, and insurmountable energy to every student at her studio. I should know. She has been my piano teacher for several years and now I am a sophomore music/pre-law major at Morehouse College. A conscientious teacher, Mrs. Jones demands the highest standards of creativity, performance, and scholarship from every child. She emphasizes the importance of going the extra mile and of giving 110 percent. She routinely inquires about our grades, and publicly displays our accomplishments and awards. Her pride in preparation, attention to detail, and high expectations is an integral part of our success. As local ensembles showcased our talent and abilities, every student was expected to compete against his or her peers with zeal and respect. Thanks to Mrs. Jones, we not only enjoyed performing but we knew we were prepared to win.
>
> In my opinion, your teacher's manual should feature Mrs. Jones as the author. She has dedicated her life to this one endeavor. She not only teaches music, but life lessons as well. On many occasions her heart-to-heart talks have guided my future. I recall two years ago when she said, "Anthony, never be caught without a dream. Those who fail to dream will fail in other areas of life as well." She recognized my passion for music and nurtured the same. Furthermore, Mrs. Jones utilizes the instructional aid "each one, teach one," whereby advanced students are given an opportunity to guide and direct their peers. For four years, I served as a piano tutor in her studio and found it to be a rich and rewarding experience. Through her example, I now understand and practice the art of giving and reaching back. More students are turned away than those blessed with the chance to study under her wing. And, for that opportunity, I will be eternally grateful. Please help me spread the word: Mrs. Jones is Charlotte's greatest teacher!
>
> Sincerely,
> Daniel Anthony Heath

In conclusion, education and music are nothing but mere tools in my hand, but when combined with high expectations, caring, and the refusal to fail, they've made a powerful combination. Sure, I can list my accomplishments and I can cite numerous achievements. But the greatest act I've ever performed has been to continuously say "Thank you" to Dr. Alston by inspiring our children and passing on the blessings so generously bestowed on me.

It's been a marvelous journey,
Clara Jones

❖   ❖   ❖

November 24, 1999
Milwaukee, WI

EVERY DAY IS A BLESSING

I have worked hard all my life. When I was young I worked like a slave—chopping cotton, picking beans, corn, and peas. I cooked and cleaned white folks' homes and hardly had time to clean my own. I scrubbed floors, washed and ironed clothes, not to mention raising eleven children. Some say that I haven't slowed down a bit. But today I do as I please. I'm a volunteer at the elementary school next to my senior citizen complex. There, I read to the children and assist the teachers. I'm also active in my church, from singing in the choir to teaching Sunday school. And I even take computer classes. Ain't that something?

I guess the hard work didn't hurt me after all. Actually, it kept me in pretty good shape. I get around by myself. I don't need a cane or a walker. My eyesight is good and I don't wear glasses. I can still hear without the use of a hearing aid. And, most important, I've got my right mind. I've made it eighy-one years and there's no need for me to ask the Lord for anything. I give Him all the praise. I need only to recognize the blessings that I've already been given.

Beauty, as they say, is in the eye of the beholder. So are blessings. A thankful eye and heart will see blessings at every turn. Every school lesson is a blessing, a chance to share all you know. Every friendship is a blessing, a chance to extend a helping hand and mend broken fences, an opportunity to give of yourself in the service of others, and a chance to make a difference. Every sermon is a blessing, the good fortune to shine your light so that it may glorify your Father in heaven, and an opportunity to pray on it. Every challenge is a blessing, an opportunity for you to overcome, a chance for you to wrestle the best out of the worst, and a chance to turn hopeless into hopeful. Take my word for it, your blessings are everywhere. Every day is a blessing—a new chance at life.

> "Enter into His gates with thanksgiving,
> and into His courts with praise" [Psalms 100:4],
> Estella Kincaid Harvey

❖   ❖   ❖

December 8, 1998
Hampton, VA

I AM BLESSED!

Work has always been the center of my life. I worked in a laundry for fifty years. It's all I've ever known. If God built the universe in six days, I worked as if I was trying to do it in five. Sometimes I would be so tired I couldn't even think straight. When I was young my parents told me, "Baby, everyone has got to do it, so you might as well be the best little worker you can be."

And that's what I did. I worked! When I started working there was no such thing as sick leave or annual leave. I worked when I felt good. I worked when I felt bad. I worked when others wouldn't. I worked when it snowed. I worked when the trolley didn't run. I made it to work in all types of weather when other folks stayed at home. As far as I can recollect there were only three days that I didn't work: To attend the funerals of my mother, father, and brother. Other than that, I never missed a beat. I have always felt that no matter what you do, take pride in what you're doing. Let your actions speak for you. Doing your job well is what the good Lord meant when He said, "Let your light shine." Why? Because you never know who's watching.

I get a tickle when I think back over the past fifty years to the world that I faced compared to the incredible world you are confronting. During my childhood I didn't know a thing about success or making money, but I was all too familiar with being poor. Today you might find it unthinkable that my generation was not able to go to the bathroom when we had to, or drink when we got thirsty, or eat when we were hungry—but nonetheless, we were eager to give thanks for our blessings. We were thankful for running water; a roof over our head; food on the table; a nice report card; young folks who would say "Yes, sir" and "Yes, ma'am"; a day without pain; money on those rainy days; the time we left the iron on and the house didn't burn down; for company on Sundays; for neighbors who would tell us when our children stepped out of line; the phone call in the middle of the night that was a wrong number and not someone calling to inform us about a death in the family; for a warm pillow underneath our head; Sunday school teachers who would hand out candy; a strong back so that we could walk erect; and a sturdy neck so that we could walk with our head held high. We were even thankful for getting old. I hope you realize some folks are gone before their time. The words "think" and "thank" were written on their hearts. Think of the gifts you possess, and thank God for his continued grace.

Now, child, let me hear you say, "I am blessed!"

Bernice Stepney

October 10, 2001
Nova Scotia, Canada

THE LETTER THAT CHANGED MY LIFE

I remember it as if it were yesterday: August 14, 2001. As hectic as it was, this is a day I will never forget. I had promised my youngest daughter that we would meet for dinner once I had completed my errands. Late that afternoon, I had one final trip to make. I stopped by my post box to gather my mail and, without thinking twice, stuffed a handful of letters into my purse before running off to our favorite restaurant. There, I met my daughter. After our waiter took our order she left for the washroom to freshen up. As I sat quietly at the table trying to catch my breath, I couldn't help but notice the envelope sticking out of my purse. In the upper left-hand corner, written in bold black letters, were the words: Community Services, Toronto. There was no need to guess its contents. I knew. For one moment in time I felt as if my world had come to a complete and sudden stop. With trembling hands I slowly opened the letter. It read in part:

Dear Ms. Atwell:

I was hoping to speak with you by telephone to receive instructions from you regarding confidential information in our files. This is not in relation to a financial matter, and it is quite important that you contact our office. I would appreciate it if you would contact me at the number above when you are able to speak freely. In the event that you are unable to reach me, please leave a detailed message and a number, and I will return your phone call at my earliest convenience.

Sincerely,
Toronto Children's Aid Society

At that moment I knew I would meet the beautiful little girl that I gave up for adoption thirty-eight years ago. As I read the letter over and over, I felt my awareness shift as if I were experiencing a dream. It took me several days to fully comprehend a journey that began in 1961.

I was seventeen when I left Nova Scotia and moved to Toronto. With little hope in the future, I quit school. There, in Ontario, I told myself that I would find the man of my dreams and lead the perfect life. It didn't take long for my hopes to be dashed. I found work in a hospital and met the man that would sweep me off my feet. I was deeply in love. As you can imagine, a few months later I got pregnant. I just knew that he would marry me, but it didn't happen. What was I thinking? I chalked the experience up to being young and naive. We continued to live together and, on August 14, 1962, I gave birth to a beautiful little girl. Times were tough and our finances were in shambles. Bearing the brunt of a gambling problem, it was hard for my boyfriend to find and keep a job. Before we knew it, I was forced to seek social assistance to help me with my baby. Gradually, we resumed our relationship, and seven months later I was pregnant again. This time I was afraid. Scared to death because even in Canada in the early sixties there was a stigma attached to single women bearing children out of wedlock. Once again, I suggested to my boyfriend that we marry and raise our children. Not only was he not interested, but after many arguments and lots of tears, he left. Here I was with a seven-month-old infant in tow and pregnant again! I was barely twenty years old. I felt abandoned, betrayed, and ashamed that I had given so much of my life and time to a man that didn't love me or his children. What was I to do? How was I to cope? The days were filled with agony. As I struggled with my decision it seemed like the weight of the world rested on my shoulders. Over the course of a few months, I came to the conclusion—what I thought to be my only option—to give this unborn child up for adoption.

After reaching this decision I waited patiently, hoping that my boyfriend would come to his senses, and run back to me with open arms saying that everything would be okay. It never happened. On April 17, 1963, I gave birth to my second child, an eight-pound baby girl. Minutes after her birth I held her in my arms and wept. This was my own flesh and blood. Months later I was called to court to sign the adoption papers and finalize the agreement. I remember holding my daughter one last time. The memory of her tiny, infant body resting on my lap was far heavier and more enduring than I thought. I couldn't stop the tears. She wore a pink dress with white sleeves, and a white border along the hem. Her hair was soft and curly; her cheeks full and round. She was a little angel, a gift from above.

Wouldn't you know it, I procrastinated. I couldn't go through with it. But when I returned to my small room and kitchen and looked at my tiny toddler, I felt overwhelmed by the prospect of bringing another child into this world. You see, I knew at some level that in my condition, I couldn't raise two children. I was young, single, possessed little education and, to top it off, I was on welfare. At that moment it didn't seem like it would be hard to put my decision behind me, or so I thought. I had to honor my commitment. I desperately wanted to give both girls a fair chance at life. The next day I returned to the courthouse and signed the papers.

Three days after this process, I phoned the Office of Social Services in Toronto and asked the caseworker if I could get my daughter back. A woman who answered the phone paused and said, "No." I then asked if I could visit her. Again, the answer was "no." She explained that once the papers are signed, most mothers feel the way I did and that my reaction was normal. She felt that I had made the best possible choice for both children. No matter how much the agency tried to assure me that all would be well, I knew that I had lost so much that day. A life. A dream. A part of myself. And a blessing from above. As days gave way to weeks, and weeks to months and years, I felt haunted to search for my child.

For the next thirty-eight years thoughts of her never left my mind. With renewed enthusiasm, I threw myself into life and began to take care of unfinished business. I returned to school, then to college, and worked to improve my professional status. I worked day and night to give my first daughter a home and to keep busy so I wouldn't remember the pain. Though I remarried in 1974 and gave birth to my third child, another little girl, the marriage ended in divorce. In 1984, I moved back to Nova Scotia where most of my family lived. There, I built a home and got involved in local politics. I ran for the post of party leader of the New Democratic Party in Nova Scotia, an election I would lose before eventually winning four years later. Between my family, constituents, and consulting practice, I was knee-deep in issues and responsibilities—and loving every minute of it. You name the cause, I got involved. You list the seminar or workshop, I signed up. Yet for all my outward success, I still sought closure. The memories of giving up my daughter and the need to find her became stronger than ever. Though I had suppressed many of the details surrounding her birth and adoption, the feeling of something missing was constant.

By 1996, the search for my child began in earnest. I knew I had to somehow pull her into my life. The first time I spoke with anyone regarding my adopted daughter occurred during a course I took on healing. As I tossed the events over in my mind everything seemed to swell up inside. For the first time, I began to share and open up with my instructor and classmates. I couldn't stop telling my story. By the end of the course an inner peace came over me and I knew that I would soon find the child that I gave up so long ago.

Call it Divine inspiration or maybe my imagination or a mother's intuition, but during that workshop I became filled with my daughter's spirit as if we were one and there was no separation between us. Something peaceful and sacred filled the air as I tried to recall every single detail regarding my daughter's birth. In disbelief, I cried when so many questions went unanswered. I had buried this secret so deep into my consciousness that I couldn't even remember my child's birthday, let alone her foster name or the doctor who delivered her. Though it wasn't easy, I never stopped asking questions.

When I read the letter from the Toronto Children's Aid Society my consciousness moved. Every possible emotion known to humanity swept through my body. I cried and shared the news with everyone. Anyone and everyone who knows me and what I've been through, wept. I had found my little girl and she had found me. In a single instant someone had just rushed in with the missing thirty-eight years of our lives. What began in 1963 ended just a few weeks ago. I finally became whole.

As of this writing I am preparing to meet that sweet little girl in the pink dress. Though we have yet to meet face-to-face, when we do words will not be enough. Each of us has dealt with our share of abandonment, pain, and loss, and this is not the time to guard our hearts. This will be the moment that our feelings will take center stage. I see myself walking up to my little girl, hugging her, and kissing her cheeks. She wrote me a letter a few weeks ago stating, in part, that an apology would not be necessary. Furthermore, she is neither angry nor bitter. Throughout her words there was a sense of familiarity, of recognition, of kinship. A strong sense of this-was-meant-to-be. Over the course of our search, we were both terrified. She was concerned that I wouldn't want to talk with her, and I was afraid she was going to hate me. She said if I had not put her up for adoption she probably would've never met her two wonderful, loving adoptive parents. She viewed my behavior as an unselfish act, which blew me away. I've said it before, this child is indeed special; where others find thorns, she sniffs for roses.

She also enclosed a picture—same hair, same eyes, same nose. We are both independent, deeply spiritual, share a warm sense of humor, and utilize a journal to record our most intimate thoughts. It seems like a miracle that we are so much alike. Our lives parallel each other in so many ways, like magnets drawn to each other. God, how I yearn to go back in time and recapture those thirty-eight years. I want to see her smile, to touch and kiss those cheeks, and to give her all of the love that rises up and overwhelms me.

Reuniting with my daughter has changed me forever. Absolutely. And for all time. It has made me look at everyone in a different light. I feel extremely blessed that God has brought us back together. I know He had a hand in the matter and that we have been reunited for some special purpose.

This experience has caused me to pause and consider, What single gift could I leave my grandchild that will light the way to a promising future? What one lesson could I pass on that will keep his feet firmly planted with the hope of added blessings to come? I've got an easy answer to those questions. Use it, and it will allow you to catch the good that lies within your reach: Never be afraid of the truth. Turn your fears into belief, and belief into knowing. You will always be protected by the love of self that truth provides. Explore your world and never fear it. God is always with you. To become the person who approaches life in this manner is to be twice blessed.

I have become whole in mind and body. For I am at peace,

Yvonne Atwell

P.S.: On September 12, 2001, I was blessed with a grandson. On September 14th, I finally connected with my little girl. In the midst of so much pain and suffering surrounding the events of September 11th, I was blessed with two births. The world is truly a beautiful place. We must understand that God, in His infinite wisdom, provides a time and place for everything to happen. And, as it should be, all is well.

November 4, 2001
Washington, DC

COUNTING MY BLESSINGS

From years of observation I am convinced that the wisest and most powerful principles for leading a life of success and inspiration have been
overlooked—even absent in institutions we hold dear. Nonetheless, I
have been blessed to be born when I was, where I was, who I was, and to
loving parents and a caring community. Each has enriched my life and
challenged my spirit. When I think of those who touched my soul and
the lessons they taught I think of purpose, love, dignity, an unwavering
faith in the giver of all life, and the need to acknowledge all blessings.
Times may change but principles don't.

Looking back, I can thank my parents—my father, a dentist, and my
mother, a schoolteacher and homemaker. God bless them. They, in turn,
were guided by their elders and surrounding community. This generation
of unknowns gave their best during their brief time. They stood tall and
faced their challenges head-on, and didn't whine or whimper. They married and raised families, and cherished the dignity that comes by earning
your own way. They weren't perfect—they only sought perfection. They
cared for each other, and fought the good fight. Though no one held the
door open for them, they made sure my avenue was wide and clear. And,
now that I am inside, my job is to keep the door from closing on you.
This is a task in which I cannot fail.

My thoughts and decisions were guided by their lessons. For unlike
those who exist only for the moment, these shining examples knew that
the only way to have meaning for today and hope for tomorrow is to go
back and draw upon the values and legacies of our families and ancestors.
The legacy passed down by my parents is priceless: a living faith reflected
by daily service, the discipline of hard work and stick-to-it-ness, and the
capacity to persist in the face of adversity. Giving up was not a part of

their vocabulary. You got up every morning and you did what you had to do. And if you stumbled along the way, you picked yourself up and you did whatever it took to get it right. Finish what you start, that's what I was taught. Period! It never occurred to Mom and Dad that any child of theirs was not going to do his or her level best. Their level best meant academic achievement, singing in the children's choir at church, displaying good manners, and being helpful to those in need. I was taught how to live and to serve and I carried these ideals forward.

Let me share all that I've learned. At age seventeen, life placed my values before me, waiting to see how I would react. At the time, I was an impetuous college student holding a head full of ideas and a briefcase full of ambition. Though I was raised in a segregated, sheltered, and structured world complete with Jack and Jill, white-gloved cotillions, and chaperoned dances, after my first day on campus it was clear to me that there were boys and girls who didn't possess many of the creature comforts I took for granted. This experience would remind me that I lived in a world divided between "have-nots" as well as "haves." It was at this moment that I decided to forgo my world of comfort and convenience and begin to forge a life with care and conviction.

At twenty-one, as a race, I knew we had a long struggle before us. I personally called every graduation class across the country "Martin's Children." I had graduated from college in June 1968, less than three months after the assassination of Dr. Martin Luther King, and two days before the death of Robert Kennedy. With my unbending desire for change, bell-bottomed jeans and love beads, I struck out into society determined to make the world a better place to live. I guess you could say I was a warrior bent on making a difference. I wanted to accomplish so much and change the world even more. And Lord knows, it wouldn't be easy. As I look back I can honestly say that of all the ailments that afflict the human spirit, racism is the most insidious. It is a silent, invisible killer that binds the soul and stifles ambition. If we are not careful it could ring the death knell for all our hopes and dreams. Nonetheless, I decided to allow the racial indifference of society to take on a different meaning and function. The ignorance of others was to serve as my teacher. I was determined to extract and retain whatever life lessons I could. I was only one but as my parents taught, sometimes one can be enough.

At twenty-four, I was charged with the responsibility of caring for my child. Moreover, I began to understand that parenting is serious business. There were times that I forced myself to remember that a child has no say regarding his or her birth. That choice was left up to me and his father, who kept that thought foremost in our mind. I cannot imagine how today's young, single mothers cope without the support we have been blessed to call upon. Today children deal with a world that bears little resemblance to the one I knew. But they also seek what every child yearns for: the knowledge that they are loved. Years from now our children won't remember how much we earned or what we did for a living; they'll remember we were there and we cared. So, never forget—mothers and fathers should and will be held accountable for their actions, maybe not by their children but certainly by the Man Above. We should not bear children until we are prepared to forsake ourselves for someone else. Women, don't even approach the sacred altar of motherhood until you are willing to give, give, and give some more. Young mothers, you will get tired. You will come to know love and frustration. That I can guarantee. Your hair won't be styled in the latest fashion, if styled at all. More often than not, your hose will have a run or two, and your shoulders will smell like sour milk. Count on it. But, believe me, when taken seriously, motherhood is the most rewarding task that you will ever undertake.

At thirty, unlike my twenties where I felt like an extended teenager, I began to confront the realities of life. I wasn't getting any younger. I bought a home, opened a modest savings account, and sought to increase what little disposable income I had by dabbling in the stock market. In short, I thought I was grown. I decided to take hold of my life.

At forty, I had fought several battles and lost many wars. I had learned the difficulties of maintaining a marriage, the power of sexism,

and the pain of divorce. As a single mother, life offered no audition for
the numerous roles I was forced to play. For years I had considered myself an old hand at living, but with so many challenges and obstacles facing me at home and in corporate America, "survivor" seemed to be a
more appropriate label. My life seemed to be working against the clock.
Even in a sexist environment where women had few rights, I played by
the rules. Though I knew the system was rigged against me and my abilities called into question daily, like other women of my day, I did what I
could and continued to survive. I couldn't worry about the lack of resources, or who or what stood in my path. I learned that you must climb
Jacob's ladder one rung at a time, and never become so discouraged that
you give up hope. I stood proud and tall, and never gave up on my
dreams. But, in all honesty, in the process of seeking a balance between
raising a child alone and climbing the corporate ladder, I had grown bitter and humble.

Age fifty proved to be the best year of my life. At this highwater
mark I discovered who I was and I liked me a lot. I learned that if you
love yourself first, everything else will fall into place. As a single woman I
learned that I live alone very well. I learned that it is not easy to find happiness in ourselves, and impossible to find it elsewhere. I learned that to
love and to be loved is the greatest joy in the world.

Speaking of joy and happiness, I love to share the following story:
One evening, my cousin and I were sitting in a restaurant eating dinner
when we were approached by the restaurant manager. He came over to
our table and said, "Your father is on the phone."

I responded, "How do you know he's my father?" The manager simply replied, "Your father told me to look for the young lady with a smile
on her face." In other words, I absolutely refuse to die unhappy.

Happiness requires that I define life on my own terms and then throw
myself into living life to its fullest. I know that happiness cannot be traveled to, possessed, worn, or consumed. Happiness cannot be found in a
new house, a fancy car, or a promising career. Nor is it for sale. When I

cannot find happiness within myself, it is useless to seek it elsewhere. Happiness is a spiritual experience of living every minute with grace and gratitude. I was placed on earth armed with a special purpose, programmed with unique talents and gifts. Happiness is not a treasure hunt but an inner treasure, and I will begin to share it. I learned patience and to always remember that things take time. I learned that the future is not what you inherit but what you create; that success is not a matter of holding a good hand but playing a poor hand well. I looked forward to climbing new hills and seeking new opportunities. And, most important, I had come to realize that the real epidemic throughout our land is what I call emotional and spiritual heart disease: the lack of love and caring. Indifference has led to the breakdown of everything that matters most— our families, our homes, our culture, and our society. Our spiritual power has been sapped by a declining moral standard that has devastated our nation as a whole. We, as a people, have increasingly abandoned time-honored virtues—values that my parents taught me more than thirty years ago—that have steadied and sustained past generations.

At fifty-five, I uncovered my role in life: To help God help people. I learned to awaken each morning with a song of praise, to give full appreciation for each new day. I learned that the simple things in life are the source of real joy. Fulfillment has nothing to do with getting. Fulfillment and contentment consist of being satisfied with the blessings already rendered. When I arise each morning, I ask God for an abundance of blessings. Why? Because a blessing is nothing more than an opportunity to do God's work. The more blessings, the more opportunity to make a difference in the lives of others. I discovered that I am rich only through what I give, and I am poor only through what I keep. My blessings cannot be computed or counted, for the true blessings of life are those treasures hidden in the reservoirs of the human heart. By counting my blessings I have turned indifference into cheerfulness and despair into laughter. I have so much for which to be grateful; so much about which to smile. All I have is all I need. My heart is grateful and I am blessed.

Whatever modest success I have managed over the course of my journey I owe not only to the lessons taught by my parents but to my neighbors, my community, and personal mentors who formed a formidable and loving network of support. Thanks, in part to their efforts, I learned life's greatest lesson: He or she who stands best, kneels most.

You have no idea how grateful I am . . .
Jane E. Smith, Ed.D.

❖   ❖   ❖

March 9, 2000
Orlando, FL

SHE WAS MOST BLESSED

This letter has taken me a long time to write because it means admitting that I am getting older, and the direction in which I am headed is much shorter than the distance from whence I've come. As the years go by and my body becomes more and more racked with pain, and my eyes dim from years of seeing the sunrise, I feel the need to tell each of you how much I love you. I have often wondered what words I might pass along that would prepare you for the years to come. Well, here are my thoughts for making your life worth living.

First, set your own agenda. What you do and what you become will depend on the choices you make. You are responsible for you. Good or bad, you're the one calling the shots. You can be a leader or a follower, but the choice is yours. Make a commitment to maintain a positive attitude and trust in the Almighty.

Second, as your great-grandmother suggested, life is a game, a game in which everyone must play. You will experience your fair share of hits as well as a strikeout or two. True joy will come when you finally hit the long one. Therefore, you can not—must not—give up. Keep swinging for the fences. Persistence is a part of the game.

Third, I cannot overemphasize the importance of education. From the day you were born until the moment your eyes will close in death, learn something new each day. Education is the vehicle that has pushed your race forward. Education makes you an equal, and only equals can compete for the rich resources of this great land.

Fourth, you must develop the "I" syndrome: I can and I will make a difference. I will not forget my mission or lose sight of my goal, no matter the frustrations or outside influences.

And fifth, you must learn to love yourself and appreciate your uniqueness. Everywhere we see folks who are starving for love, famished for affection, for someone—anyone—to appreciate them. On every hand we see men and women who possess material comfort, who are able to satisfy nearly any wish, and yet they hunger for love. They seem to have plenty of everything but affection. I suggest we try a different approach and use God's instrument for transforming the world. There is no one like you nor will there ever be anyone exactly like you. You have been given unique talents and skills. You must never allow anyone to determine your values, control your thoughts, or chip away at your self-esteem. You must never allow anyone to rob you of your ability to love. As you experience your personal walk, I beg of you, learn and apply this one great life lesson: When living life, lead with your heart.

I've lived a long and fulfilling life but if I fail to see another day, bury what I am about to say deep into your spirit. I want you to know how special you are—not only to me, specifically, but to the world in general. I adore you and accept you exactly as you are. I want and expect nothing more from you than your right to be happy and fulfilled as God so intended. I, in turn, will try to become the best person I can, hoping that you will never view me as a burden or feel obliged to care for me in any way. There is nothing that you will ever do that will disappoint or discourage me or make my love for you wane. You have my unconditional love and the knowledge that my feelings will never change. As I complete this letter I am reminded of the simple prayer that hangs on my bedroom wall. As the story goes, the author was an unknown soldier during the Civil War. I have adapted and added to his original words as if they were my own. I trust you will take the time to memorize this humble plea:

She asked for strength to do great things,
She was given affliction so that she might do better things.
She asked for riches so she might be happy,
She was given poverty so she might be wise.
She asked for power so she might be the praise of women,
She was given weakness so she might fill the need of God.
She had received nothing she had asked for—but all that she had hoped for.
Her prayers seemed unanswered but she was most blessed.

Thank you for the love and joy you've brought into my life,
Kattie J. Adams

❖   ❖   ❖

November 30, 2001
Oakland, CA

BLESS THE LIVES OF OTHERS

We bless the life around us far more than we realize. Many simple, innocent acts that we take for granted can affect those around us in profound ways: the unexpected phone call, the willingness to listen, the smile of recognition, the warm meal and soft blanket, not to mention the helping hand. I've tried to touch the lives of many, especially those who feel abandoned, rejected, and lonely. I've tried to feed and clothe their bodies, help them regain what little self-esteem they have left, and inspire them to persevere in the face of suffering. I've tried to offer them hope, love, and the knowledge that someone cares. I've tried to live my life as a proclamation of the gospel.

I was born eighty years ago—and it would probably take me eighty years to tell my entire story—in New Orleans, Louisiana. My mama and daddy were sharecroppers, and I worked every square inch of our farm. When I say we were dirt poor, I mean we were dirt poor! No shoes, no clothes, no running water. Mama died when I was five years old so I was forced to work even harder. I quit school after the second grade to pick cotton and help raise my five brothers and sisters. By age fourteen I had married and given birth to the first of my twelve children. But by the time I had my ninth child, my marriage turned sour. Neither me nor the children could take the abuse any longer. So, one day, me and my daughters packed all of our belongings in a pillow case and took a train clear across the country to live with my sister in Oakland, California. There, I found a job working sixteen hours a day as a domestic. Without the ability to read or write it seemed like a mop and bucket were the only tools that could fit my hand. And the pay? One dollar per hour. A year later, I was able to bring my boys out west to live with us.

Then one night in 1980—two decades ago, in the dead of winter—I got a wake-up call that would change my life forever. The good Lord woke me up from a sound sleep with a haunting question: How can I lie in my warm, comfortable bed knowing there are hungry mothers and children sleeping on the cold pavement? I knew what I had to do. From that moment my mission in life was to help the hungry and homeless. Initially, no one wanted to support my efforts or give food to the homeless. To compound matters, my family thought I had lost my mind. And, if that was not enough, when I drove to our local farmer's market and told the manager what I wanted to do, he shook his head in disbelief and replied, "Lady, do you know how many people come down here begging each day?"

I said, "I know. But if you just help one time I promise you, I won't be back." That was twenty-one years ago. I was forced to take matters into my own hands.

The following Saturday, I decided to get the ball rolling. I cashed my social security check—$236—and began cooking in my kitchen. When I finished, me and a few neighbors and volunteers loaded up my old station wagon and drove to a local park. There, we set up tables and provided hot meals for more than five hundred people. Whoever assisted me, I insisted that they serve the homeless with dignity. "Serve them as if you would serve yourself," I instructed. "Never look down your nose at anyone. Use shiny silverware and clean napkins. Throw a colorful tablecloth over the table. Serve them like they're somebody special."

Everybody has a story to tell. Society calls these people buggy pushers. These are everyday folks—no better, no worse than you or I—who just fell through the cracks, and you and I have been placed here to help them get back on their feet. I've seen people from all walks of life who are down on their luck, from auto workers to Silicon Valley ex-millionaires. If we don't treat each other with dignity and love here on earth, we might as well hang it up talking about going to Heaven. Over the next few weeks, and with much persistence, $5 and $10 checks, and occasional bags of canned goods and clothing trickled in. But it was those sloppy joe sandwiches that I fixed with my social security check for two straight years that got us on our way.

Well, much has changed over the past twenty years. Four churches now take turns cooking and serving dinners under my guidance. And, in addition to serving home-cooked holiday meals every Thanksgiving and Christmas, we now provide thousands of families with a turkey and enough groceries to last several days. Last Thanksgiving hundreds of volunteers—from schools, churches, the Oakland Raiders football team, and even a ministry in China—formed an assembly line to sort and bag canned food, thousands of loaves of bread, pies, and other fixings, and gave away eight thousand donated turkeys. Why, we even clothe and feed people in Nairobi, Kenya, as well as the brokenhearted in the former

Soviet Union. I'm just overjoyed and proud that my mission has touched so many generous hearts.

Today, it seems everybody is calling, inviting me to speak to their group, school or business. Imagine that. Just a short time ago I was just me with my second-grade education. Now I'm speaking all over the world! I've received more than three hundred awards and honors from the White House on down. But it has never been about me or about what I've done. If I wasn't doing anything you would've never heard of me. Many go through life with their eyes fixed on some distant goal, on something they don't need and probably can live without. On their way they pass opportunities to lift and bless the lives of others, a chance to scatter seeds of love and kindness. But they see them not. Oh, how pitiful the sight. No one will live long in the world's memory who does nothing more than selfishly chase the almighty dollar. When will we learn that heart wealth is real wealth, and that money in itself is worthless when compared to the currency of love? Fame, wealth, position, honor—these values have little to do with real success. The most successful man that ever lived was despised of men, and so poor that "He had nowhere to lay His head" [Luke 9:58]. And, when they finally arrive at their destination, sadly they discover that they have gained the world but lost their soul. Their hearts are as dry as dust. They have gained what they sought, but at the expense of all that sweetens and enhances. My Bible urges me to seek a larger mission, one that includes sincerity of the heart, longing of the soul, and the willingness to bless my fellow man, no matter where I may find him. So if he is in the gutter, he belongs to God. If I find him in the palace, he's a child of the Almighty. If he is black, brown, yellow, or white, it doesn't matter. We are all branches on the same tree. If he is found wearing tattered clothing, sleeping under commuter rail tracks, I am no better than he. But for the grace of God, there go I.

No, I am not a scholar nor a celebrity. I'm just a little black woman who's been blessed by the Lord, trying her best to pass this blessing on to others. It's about the Christ within me, all that I am, all that I ever will be. The greatest joy of my life is to feed God's children. Such a legacy will enrich more than all the millions one could amass.

> What are we living for, if we are not living for each other?
> Mother Mary Ann Wright

❖   ❖   ❖

FINAL THOUGHTS ON COUNT IT ALL JOY!

May 16, 1998
Atlanta, GA

I'm convinced, the waste of life lies in the love not given, the power not used, and the blessings that we fail to acknowledge.

Vivian E. Thomas

❖   ❖   ❖

November 26, 1997
Louisville, KY

You will not be in heaven until heaven is in you. It's good to have money and the trappings that money can buy. But it is good, too, to check up once in a while to make sure you haven't lost sight of the sacred pleasures that no amount of money can purchase.

Dorothy Scott

June 25, 1998
Brooklyn, NY

There's something that even Bill Gates, with all of his billions, cannot purchase or replace: peace of mind.

Marione Nixon

⬥   ⬥   ⬥

April 19, 2000
Indianapolis, IN

Each week my mother gave me and my sister an allowance: one dime. We were told to tithe one-tenth for offering in church. We never complained. After all, we had nine pennies left to buy candy. I guess my sister and I thought we were rich. As I now look back, I can see how rich we really were.

Lenora Grissom

⬥   ⬥   ⬥

November 2000
Philadelphia, PA

My grandmother didn't say anything that I didn't already know. It was how she said it. "Be mindful of your blessings," she explained. "You didn't earn them. There's nothing special about you. They were given to you by the God of all things. You, in turn, must show gratitude by never losing sight of the human element. Do the right thing. Make a contribution. Fill a void when least expected." My grandmother's teaching reinforced one of her favorite biblical verses: The Sermon on the Mount. There is a peace in knowing that a great leveling is coming, that every valley shall be exalted and every mountain and hill made low; that people who lead lives of challenge and heartache possess opportunities for greater growth than those who are graced with fortune and ease. It is important that each of us keep pushing, to search for the good, to strive and endure to the end, to live in harmony with our fellow traveler, to help make this world a better place for those living as well as for future generations.

Gertrude Jordan

Chapter Five

Love

Letter

ccording to these black grandmothers, love is the supreme work for which we've been called. Our world is not a playground but a classroom. Life is not a holiday but an education. And the one eternal lesson? Learn to love. Why has love been called the greatest of these? Because love is the common denominator to life; the magic potion of the soul. It has been known to weaken the mighty and strengthen the weak. It can wipe a tear from a sad face as well as inspire an overmatched army. It can make you lose your senses and, in times of desperation, be the only thing that makes sense. Love keeps the sick alive and makes the healthy feel sick. It is love that stiffens our back, and it is love that makes us tremble in fear. It is the be-all and end-all. We cannot see it, yet it is the light by which we live. We cannot hear it, yet it is the still, small voice that drives us on. We cannot touch it, yet we can feel it beating within our heart. We cannot hold it, yet in times of great stress and sorrow it may be the only sure thing we can cling to. This is the power of love. So, their advice to me—and to each of us—is to try love's way. In all our affairs, try love's way. Our lives are filled with opportunities to be larger instead of smaller; thoughtful and caring, instead of rude and careless; and to love a little more and loathe a little less. By these small acts we will brighten our image in the minds of others. By our actions we will teach humanity's greatest duty.

Greet this day with love in your heart, you who are worn out by a cold, insensitive world and you who struggle every day through discord and disappointment just to nudge ahead. If you have not yet tried love as a principle, as a life philosophy, begin now. Love warms all hearts just as the rays of the sun soften the coldest clay.

Try love's way, it is the cure-all, the Christ remedy that raises humanity to a higher standard. Try love's way, you who seem so lost; you who've allowed worry to deplete your strength and sap your birthright—the abundant life. You've crossed bridges before you have even approached them and you lie awake at night brooding over difficulties that will never come to pass. What has fear and worry ever done? Has worry ever added to your well-being? Has it increased your comfort and happiness? Has it ever solved a problem? Turn to a higher source. From Genesis to Revelation, love is an unending refrain: "Let not your heart be troubled, neither let it be afraid" (John 14:1).

Try love's way, you whose home is filled with tension and strife, whose marriage and family bear the emotional scars of friction, failure, pain, and regret. Home is where the heart is, and it's time for a heart-to-heart talk. You've birthed your children, but you did not bless them. You never disciplined, and now you face disaster. You paid the rent, but you did not pay attention. You've never been devoted, and now you face divorce. Without love, communication, and caring, a house is not a home. Try love for every trouble, for every hurt and sorrow. Allow love to shine in your eyes, unwrinkle your brow, bring a smile to your lips, and an echo to your voice. See if it does not cast a warm spirit over those who abide within.

Try love's way, you who are living the life. By popular standards you've got it all to-gether. You're superbly equipped—a fine education, a top job, and plenty of everything. You think you've reached the height of your financial blessings. You're at the peak of your game. But a peak is only visible after the decline that follows. You're the picture of success. But looks can be deceiving. Underneath, the canvas tells a different story. Is it true? Are you coldhearted and mean-spirited? A slave to the dollar? Are you wrapped up in a me-first attitude, only looking out for number one? How low will you stoop? How many toes will you step on to ensure your position and power? It's nice to be important but it's important to be nice. Have you ever wiped a tear from a sad face? Neither life nor love can be meas-ured in the attainment of material possessions. Success should be applauded but only love should be worshiped. We imprison the burglar for breaking into our homes and stealing our belongings. But what shall we do with you—the self-centered soul who uses his talents to trample the very people that hold you in such high esteem? Give love a try. Whoever uplifts civilization, though he or she dies penniless, is rich. Great buildings have never been erected on uncertain foundations. Great causes have never been brought to success by unloving lead-ers. Love has always been, and always will be, at the root of any meaningful endeavor. Yours will be a better world when the power of love replaces the love of power. The praise and love you give to others will melt away that cold exterior and reveal the spirit of a man who knows who he should be.

You've tried the revenge way, the hatred and grudge method, the jealousy approach, the worry and anxiety plan, the silent treatment, the eye-for-an-eye routine, as well as bullying and browbeating, and these methods have tortured you all the more. Why, you've even tried law and the courts to settle your troubles and disputes, and look where it has gotten you. Why not give love a try? Love your enemies and they will become your friends. Treasure your friends and they will become brothers and sisters. Embrace the wealthy and they will become humble. Honor the humble and they will become divine. In all your affairs, try love's way.

❖　❖　❖

June 25, 1999
Chicago, IL

LOVE IS AWESOME

It is not important who you love or what you love, but rather that you love. For love is awesome!

Yvette Ridley

❖　❖　❖

January 8, 1998
Greensboro, NC

LOVE THEM UNCONDITIONALLY

Though I choose to share my words, this letter is written in complete anonymity. Continue to read and, hopefully, you will understand why.

I have suffered from deep emotional scars throughout my childhood which I've struggled with every day of my life. I felt that my parents did not love me simply because they never told me. There was no hugging, no touching, and no affection of any kind ever shown. Naturally, I felt inadequate, unworthy, and, as a result, I carried a great deal of emotional trauma throughout my life. Though today, I'm happy to report, I'm much better.

As I reflect, I now realize my parents suffered from the same troubling experience during their childhood. Love was never expressed. So what am I trying to say? Parents, family, friends, please take the time to show each other—and especially your children—that you love them unconditionally, and appreciate everyone for who they are. Kiss your children, hug them, tell them how much you love them. Spend quality time with those that matter most. Their lives will be much more productive and so will yours.

Love can alter the most stagnant heart,
Anonymous

❖   ❖   ❖

March 24, 2000
Washington, DC

LOVE IS DIVINE

It is impossible to overestimate the value of love. There is nothing love cannot alter, nothing that love cannot fix. Love enriches, sweetens, and soothes the soul. Love is the power in each of us that is Divine. Love produces sunshine wherever it goes, and it shuts out winter's chill. Love sheds a tear in times of celebration and sorrow. Love is a tender word of sympathy to the discouraged and the disheartened. Love is the blanket and the slice of bread placed in the hand of the homeless and the hungry. Love is the security that children seek, the glue that binds a marriage,

and the oil that prevents friction in the home. Be not afraid, and never
hate another. There is nothing so needed and sought as love.

Write your name onto the hearts of humanity through acts of love,
Diana Onley-Campbell

✦   ✦   ✦

May 24, 2000
Atlanta, GA

LOVE YOURSELF

My Dearest Children:

Isn't it written somewhere that love is the most simple of acts? You
would be shocked how few people bother to express it. When it comes to
living in our fast-paced world, I am not concerned about the quality of
life that so many take for granted. I am not concerned with recent trends
that painstakingly point out how good or how bad our lives are becoming. It makes little difference to me of my or anyone's ability to sit before
a computer and talk to five billion souls across the globe or by simply
punching a few buttons, purchase anything and everything under the sun.
I can live without it. I wouldn't give two cents regarding how many sta-
tions I can receive on my portable TV—though I do enjoy the religious
programs. I could care less that I can fly from New York to Paris in less
than five hours. I have no need to rush because I've got plenty of time. I
wouldn't lose a minute of sleep if I ever had to walk into a bank rather
than use an automatic teller machine. Personally, I like the human touch.
I've made it this far with it and I see no sense in changing now.

As bad as crime is today, I am not too worried about the mugger, the
thief, the crook, the swindler, the burglar, the embezzler, the drug dealer

or those who come stealing in the night. Yes, I know they are out there but they're not the source of my fears. Furthermore, I am not overly concerned with anybody or any man—specifically any one individual or person, such as the boss man, the con man, or the pusher man. They may knock me down, run me down, or hold me down, but they can't hold me back. There is no need for any of the above to capture my attention. Of themselves, they are powerless, and merit little concern. However, if there is anything that is worthy of my respect and demands my concern, and that I must constantly confront and wrestle with each and every day is the answer to the question: Do I love myself?

To a large extent, the foundations of emotional well-being are formed during childhood. Those with backgrounds similar to mine are well aware of that truth. We know what it feels like to be filled with self-doubt. How we yearn to be loved and wanted. This testimony was written and read by me at the funeral of my mother who gave me up for adoption. She died nearly three months to the day after my foster mother passed. I pray that my words will be of help to those who, like me, drifted through life feeling neglected and deprived. I had to accept the reality that love and approval from others would never manifest until I embraced it from within.

JUST FOR YOU, MOM

I want to say to my mother, and any others
Time is moving steady, God knew that you were ready
I am who I am because of your obedience in a personal way.
I didn't understand then, like I do now why I am that special child.
I told you before you left this earth,
I love you, I forgive you, and I thank God you permitted my birth.
You had a choice—allow me to live or die,
You chose life, and now I see why.
So I won't say goodbye . . . that's too long

Instead I'll shout "Hallelujah," and rejoice in song.
I love you, Mom, but the Master loved you more,
Rest in peace until I knock upon Heaven's door.

Lovenia T. Wamget

❖   ❖   ❖

April 29, 1997
Atlanta, GA

THE GREATEST OF THESE IS LOVE

Here is my recipe for wholesome living:

(1) Faith: Believe in God and His word.
(2) Patience: Prove yourself worthy and be morally upright.
(3) Charity: Be willing to care for and share with those less fortunate.
(4) Love: Practice Godliness and love unconditionally.

All godly men and women who have walked this planet know this to be true: Love is the ideal and the dream of every person, for in love were our souls conceived, and in love is our destiny to express. We are fulfilled when we are in love, and somehow empty without it. It is the very purpose of our being, and the vision held by the man upstairs when we sprang from the womb. Love is the one word that contains the same meaning in every language. Heads may differ but hearts never.

Faith, hope, and charity, but the greatest of these is love
[I Corinthians 13:13],
Willie P. Hunt

February 4, 2001
Baltimore, MD

A SINGLE WORD

To my children and grandchildren:
   My thoughts, in a single word: Love.

If only we could love enough, everything else would fall into place,
Doretha Gilliam

❖   ❖   ❖

March 12, 2001
Staunton, VA

LOVE IS AS SIMPLE AS ABC

When I think of you, an enormous feeling of boundless love rushes over
me. As I recall the moments of your births, my spirit instantly fills with
pride. Each time I had hoped for a miracle and received it. Soft of voice
and strong on conviction, it has been a joy to watch you evolve. You are
six souls with one heart.

My love for you is genuine and without limits. I feel privileged that
God chose me to be your mother and grandmother. For you, I only wish
the best in this life and beyond. So how then shall you live? It is my hope
that you will:

   A: Grow to believe in yourself and your destiny, and allow the power
      of love to permeate your spirit.
   B: Give of yourself by passing your love on to others. Be an example

of God's love and peace. Now, more than ever, people need hugs, smiles, and sympathetic ears. Fulfill the needs of the heart.

C: Love and trust in God. For God is love. He will prove to be that strong gust of wind the moment you decide to spread your wings.

There have been many who've written books regarding how to succeed and how to live your dreams. Everyone seeks to be happy and successful—that's life's one common denominator. In addition to my advice above, I urge you to seek these books out and apply the advice that lies within. However, I must warn you. Defining success can be a difficult task. Amid fame, fortune, and the trappings of success, any blueprint that does not include prayer, disciplined Bible study, and a spiritual relationship is poorly mapped. The goal is not life on earth, but life everlasting. Yes, my love for you is special, but God's love is perfect. Though my love is limited to this world and life, God's love is timeless. His faith in you is fixed, and His grace and undying devotion is too vast and too broad to be confined to this measly sheet of paper.

My favorite song, "If I Could," sung by Regina Belle, expresses a mother's love for her children. This is a song the strong heart sings. If I could, I would be with you always, sharing my love, wrapping my arms around you. If I could, I would hold your hand as you stretch and strain to reach your dreams. And, if I could, I would allow my love to shape your days and reveal the beauty and true meaning of life.

May my words lift and move you from the petty to the profound,
Rosemary Wynne McCauley

January 1999
Hampton, VA

LOVE IS . . .

In February 1999, Lord willing, I will see my sixty-ninth birthday. For fifty-three years I've been married to the same man. God has also blessed me with four loving children. I knew nothing about marriage when I said, "I do." I came from a poor family, but I had the good fortune to be raised by a relative who loved me dearly.

I always placed my family first. My children never had to come home to an empty house. There were always three hot meals a day waiting for them, even on weekends. How did I say "I love you?" Let me count the ways: Eat your vegetables; always wear clean underwear; clean your room; hold hands when crossing the street; play nice with the other children; be home before dark; and mind your manners. A little love goes a long way but a lot of love lasts forever. Love is there when you need it. Love is the phone call to say everything is alright. Love takes your temperature when you're sick. Love waits at the airport for the last flight to come in. Love gets up in the middle of the night. Love is staying at home. Love is the helping hand that gives its last dollar. Love goes out in all types of weather. Love walks a step behind. Love goes the extra mile and expects nothing in return. Love can work magic, turning natural-born enemies into brother's keepers. Love doesn't keep score and it measures not the cost or the sacrifice. Love is never fifty-fifty—it's total commitment. Love sets an example. Love disciplines, and sometimes it says "No."

I always felt that God placed me on this earth to be a mother and a wife, and, you know what—I'm a darn good one! If you have to tell your children that you love them, you probably don't.

Love is a more perfect way,
Carrie V. Garrow

January 10, 2001
Decatur, GA

THE MARVELOUS POWER OF LOVE

Talk about busy, this was a crucial time in my life. I was up to my eye-balls with things to do. Everyone seemed to be counting on me for physi-cal and emotional support. With a disabled husband, three small children that had to be shuffled to school each day, and a full-time job, my plate was full. We'd been married for nearly eight years, and though still in his fifties, cancer and open-heart surgery had knocked the wind out of him, forcing my husband to go on disability. I was about to settle on my sofa and catch my breath, when the phone rang. It was my sister. As I look back, I now know what it took for her to make that call. She was tired, alone, and had nowhere to turn. "Would you be willing to take a baby?" she sobbed.

"A baby!" I shot back. "Who in the world is having a baby?"

"My daughter," she replied. I should have expected as much. For most of her adult life my niece was lost in a world of drugs, crime, and sorry relationships with one no-good man after another. Here was a young woman, darn near knocking on thirty who, for all intent and pur-pose, had left her three small children with their grandmother to care for. When I found out she was pregnant, I said to myself, "What else is new?" It was hard to feel sorry for her.

My husband is not one that is easily riled up but I will never forget his response. "A baby?" he asked in disbelief. "You can't be serious! We are in no position to take care of a baby!" He didn't know the particulars and he didn't care to know. I, on the other hand, had more questions than answers. The bottom line was that I was the only one working and he was drawing social security benefits. For the next three days we considered every inch of our budget and wondered how in the world we could feed another mouth. Next, we questioned our sanity—newborn parents at our age, you must be joking! Finally, we prayed as if there was no tomorrow. The following morning we phoned my sister with the news she had hoped to hear: Yes, we would take the baby. Unfortunately, we were a day late. My niece had given birth the night before to a healthy baby girl named Portia, who was immediately shipped off to foster care.

Phone calls to the Dekalb and Cobb county social services divisions revealed that our quest to become Portia's foster parents would not be an overnight process. In fact, between foster parent classes (imagine that, me taking parenting classes, but you do what you've got to do) and social worker home visits, by the time all the i's had been dotted and the t's crossed, it would be nearly one year before me, my husband, my sister, and Portia's mother would stand before a judge to sign the appropriate papers. But before we did, my niece had another confession. She was pregnant. Again! At least a month and a half. I swear, it floored everyone in the room. Dumbfounded, the judge didn't know what to do or say. In a sheepish way he asked if me and my husband would be willing to take custody of this forthcoming child, in order to keep the children together. Without hesitation, we said, "Yes."

It would be more than three years before we would ever see or hear from my niece again. The state had terminated her parental rights. Portia was four and Rose Marie was three, born when her mother was about to OD on a cocaine binge. The children have adapted quite well. You'd be surprised what you can do when love and the Lord are at the heart of your home. One day when we were about to sit down to dinner, I received one last phone call. On the line was a social worker from the Detox division of Dekalb county. My niece was in court-ordered rehab and, you guessed it, she was due any day. James, her sixth child, was only seven days old when we picked him up from the child services facility.

Today, I am the mother of six beautiful, healthy children. Three of my own and three adopted, but all gifts from above, and each a blessing. How do we manage? I'm still trying to figure that out. You work, you sleep, and you try to keep up. Sure, we rake and scrape—child, I know how to stretch a dollar—but I admit, the Lord plays a major role. Each weekday begins with bowls of cereal and a helping of Scripture. It's been quite a journey. How did the experience change me? That's what everyone wants to know. I discovered that whenever you make a decision with love and kindness, it's usually the right decision. I learned that everyone could use a prayer. I learned that singing "Blessed Assurance" can lift your spirits all day. I learned that every day you should reach out and touch some-one—we all love the human touch. I learned that when you share, you always wind up with more. And, most important, I uncovered the marvelous power of love. Love lightens heavy burdens, sweetens the hardest labor, turns revenge into forgiveness, and warms the coldest heart. There's no power in the universe greater than love, and no act more im-portant than loving. What you receive in return for love and hope is priceless.

He's been with me every step of the way,
Ella Goolsby

❧   ❧   ❧

January 17, 2001
Decatur, GA

LOVE IS THE BEST REMEDY

The public school system said my grandson has attention deficit disor-der—fancy words for bad behavior. As a result, he was placed on Ritalin to calm him down. I hate that stuff. I can tell when he's on it because he comes home walking around like a zombie. Against the school's wishes I took him off the medication. Seems like the principal was calling every five minutes telling me to come pick him up. As soon as we got home I would whip his butt. But spanking was not the answer, either. He would simply dry his eyes and go about his business, acting the fool. But one day I tried a different approach. I began to hug him and embrace him, and tell him how proud I was to be his grandmother. I told him that he is a bright and special child—God's child—destined to do great things. And don't you know, he seemed to change overnight. Months later, his teachers and guidance counselor called me and wanted to know what in the world was going on. I told them that we tried drugs and beatings to no avail. But this time I was determined to love the Devil out of him. I haven't had any problems since.

> Love is the best remedy. Give it in large doses,
> Millie Turnipseed

❖   ❖   ❖

March 25, 1999
Chicago, IL

A LOT OF LOVE LASTS FOREVER

For my daughters, granddaughter, and my granddaughters to come,

I thank God for allowing me to be your mother as well as your grandmother. As the story goes, you know how I prayed for a daughter during each of my pregnancies. Well, obviously, God heard my prayers. In return for these blessings, I feel it is appropriate for me to provide you with a few tools as you make this magnificent journey through life:

- Walk tall and remember your ancestors, for they are the cause of your blessings. Your presence is a present to the world.
- Life is precious. Take the time to wish upon a star. Live a life of serenity, not a life of regrets.

- Respect yourself and others, and always choose your friends wisely.
- Hold tight to your culture, it will keep you in balance.
- Count your blessings, not your troubles. Be a blessing to others. It's amazing how much an individual's hearing improves when he or she hears a word of praise.
- "You can do all things through Christ who strengthens you" (Luke 18:27). Do ordinary things in extraordinary ways. Never let go of His hand.
- Be honest, so your children will know honesty. Be kind, so your children will learn kindness. Be faithful, so your children will walk by faith.
- Never expect love in return, just wait for it to grow in the heart of another. If it doesn't, be content it grew in yours.

When you leave this world, you will be asked to give an accounting for all that you have done. You will be asked the following questions: Why are you here? And, what is the one desire that you wish most from life? More so than a comfortable home, fine clothes and the friendship of others? More than peace and tranquility; more than education and opportunity for your children; more than money on rainy days or the ability to give to others? What is the one perfect gift that will give your life satisfaction and meaning?

You might not know it yet, but the answer is to love and to be loved. To be able to arrive at your final days with few regrets; to be free of pain and suffering; to glance back and see a life well lived. If you can love and be loved, yours will be the world of your dreams.

A little love goes a long way, but a lot of love lasts forever,
Linda C. Gresham

March 26, 1998
Newport News, VA

THE UNENDING LOVE OF FRIENDS

Friends. They enrich. They annoy. They help. They hinder. They can be
your toughest critic, and yet, they care. True, friends can't solve all of
life's problems or fears but they can listen, serve as a sounding board, and
together the two of you can find solutions. A friend may not be able to
prevent you from failing, but she can hoist you up once you've stumbled,
or even break your fall. A friend may not be able to keep your heart from
hurting, but she can cry with you and help pick up the pieces. Above all,
friends are family. Here is a revealing story on the nature of friendship:

Ann and I were, and are, best friends. Joined at the hip since high
school, we were inseparable. You didn't see one without the other. We
shared the same hopes, dreams, and ambitions. Amazingly, after our high
school graduation, we served as maid of honor at our respective weddings, and moved to suburbia to launch similar careers and start families.
We even had the same number of children. If Ann started a sentence, I
would finish it. We were that close. And then our relationship changed,
drastically.

Several years ago on Christmas Eve, Ann asked to borrow money. I
agreed to loan her the money with the stipulation that she repay me at a
specified time. Now, I'm not one to turn my back on a friend in need nor
am I a penny pincher, but I've never been in the habit of throwing my
money away either. Though I love Ann to death, she has an irritating history of borrowing money and either paying back in dribs and drabs, or
not paying at all. This was not the first time I loaned her money, but I decided, it was certainly going to be the last. True to form, once I loaned her
the money days turned into weeks, and weeks became months before Ann
lived up to her commitment. I, on the other hand, did and said nothing.
Then, out of the blue, I received a note from her thanking me for helping

her out. A check was enclosed. With my money firmly in hand I was glad to put this little episode behind me. But my peace quickly withered. Less than two days later, her check was returned to me by my bank marked "stopped." Shocked and confused, I didn't know what to do but calling was out of the question. From there, things between us got messy and our relationship ended—at least for the next eighteen years.

Circumstances moved us into different circles, and for nearly two decades, we ignored each other and only sent regards through mutual friends. Basically, we stopped speaking. But fate, however, would have nothing of it. During a social gathering we were literally forced to speak and acknowledge each other's presence. In an attempt to catch up on old times we gathered the nerve to address the issue. It turned out that Ann knew nothing of the bounced check! Furthermore, she thought the debt had been repaid years ago, and, that I held a grudge because she was late honoring her commitment. I, as you can imagine, wondered why my best friend wanted nothing more to do with me. After all, it was I who loaned her the money in the first place. What a colossal misunderstanding! Ashamed and embarrassed, we held each other as we did so many times in the past, drying each other's tears.

Fortunately, our story has a happy ending. Here we are, real friends again. The bitterness, anger, and resentment are gone, partly due to lost time and to our revelation. Wiser and older, we know we need each other. In matters of the heart our friendship has deep roots. Having lost it once, we vowed to be twice as careful not to lose our friendship again.

I pray that you benefit from my experience. I hope that you will grow to cherish your friends because they are both fragile and priceless. There are many types of friends. Some are closer than others. But, no matter what, friends are friends forever. Though the shapes of friendships certainly change, soul connections never end.

Now, I've got to run. Ann and I have some catching up to do!
Eleanor F. Weekes

November 30, 2001
Junction City, KS

LOVE KNOWS NO COLOR (I)

You think that I have all the answers. If you only knew! Sometimes grandmothers can be frail and fragile, but also strong and resilient. Just like you. I have known fear, anger, and sadness. My heart has been broken and I have known moments when the hand of God seemed to be on my shoulder. I have wept tears of sorrow and tears of joy. I have carried others when I barely had the strength to carry myself.

I guess you could call it love at first sight. My husband and I met in the spring of 1949, after the war. We married a year and a half later, as soon as the law would allow. That's right, it took a public law to approve of our marriage. You see, I'm Japanese and my husband is black. We exchanged our vows not too far from the place of my birth in Yokohama, Japan. To compound our difficulties, at the time I could barely speak a word of English. Over the course of the next fifty-one years that would change. While my English dramatically improved, I taught my family a fair amount of Japanese. Today, one of my grandchildren speaks fluent Japanese. Now I know what you're thinking. Yes, we had some idea as to the pitfalls of an interracial marriage. Yes, we knew some parts of the country would be less than warm regarding our relationship. And, yes, some even said our marriage didn't stand a chance, but try telling that to our four grown children and six grandchildren. No matter the language or culture, there's a common denominator that stood the test of time: The love my husband and I share for each other.

A successful marriage is built on trust, love, and, when times get tough, the ability to lean on each other. Any marriage must be handled with care. From day one, we made up our mind that our marriage meant forever and nothing was going to stop us. Our marriage was always viewed as the most sacred of partnerships, not an agreement or a contract, but a spirit-filled union under the watchful eyes of our Creator. My husband and I came from backgrounds where life was a team effort and the unity of the family was the collective goal. Our wedding vows were unconditional. Now before you ask, there's nothing magical about our relationship. Oh, sure, we've had our ups and downs, and our moments or two. But they've been just that—moments. Thankfully, we've always been able to weather the storms—times are no harder or more difficult than what we make them out to be. Marriage is just like gaining interest in the bank: If you don't put nothing in, you won't get nothing out. And to be honest, I think a big reason why our marriage has lasted this long is because I can cook a mean pot of greens and black-eyed peas with the best of them!

God bless,
Shige Graves

♢   ♢   ♢

September 12, 2000
Atlanta, GA

DRYING HER SON'S TEARS AFTER A
RELATIONSHIP WENT AWRY

Dear Sweetheart,

I awoke this morning with you on my mind. I've got so many things to worry about but you are always my number one priority. It hurts to love someone and not to be loved in return, but it is more painful to love someone and never find the courage to let that person know how you feel. Maybe God wants us to meet a few wrong people before meeting Mr. or Ms. Right. That way when we do meet the right person we will be so appreciative for the gift. It can be so trying to meet someone who means a lot to you, only to discover in the end that it was never meant to be. When that occurs, it's best to simply end the relationship.

As you know, I've been through the wars of life, especially in the relationship department. After the crying, after the blaming and finger pointing, I have found the best way to cope is to dive into work. When life has me pinned against the ropes, keeping busy is the best medicine. I love the saying: "Keep your mind on your work, don't let life work on your mind." You have so much going for you, and I want you to remember all of your wonderful attributes: you're sensitive, caring, charming, smart, talented, and, have I failed to mention handsome? These qualities will keep you moving in the right direction. Bitterness, anger, loathing, and self-pity, ultimately, will drive you away from your goals and the relationship that matters most: you and The Lord. Every day when you arise, shake off any temptation to belittle yourself. Instead, take it one step at a time. Think of a way to improve your situation for that day—then do it! Trust me. You will feel empowered.

I love you, and it hurts me to know you are hurting. All things in life have a beginning, a middle, and an end. Sometimes love begins with a smile, grows with a kiss, and ends with a tear. But nothing goes on forever, and this too shall pass. Don't worry, the Man upstairs has a way of evening the score. It's true. We don't know what we've got until we lose it, but it is equally true that we don't know what we've been missing until it arrives. You will find your perfect soul mate.

"He shall wipe every tear from your eye" [Revelation 21:4],
Lezlie R. Bishop

May 3, 2000
Indianapolis, IN

HAVE I TAUGHT YOU TO LOVE?

I am a member of Light of the World Christian Church under the leadership of Bishop T. Garrott Benjamin, Jr. Dr. Benjamin asked the grandmothers in his congregation to reply to the question: If given the chance, what would you tell your children or the next generation about life? Since that Sunday service, I've done little except to kneel in prayer and consider my Pastor's request. I just hope and pray my response helps.

The world, it is said, is always searching for men and women who know the Lord: men and women who are honest as the day is long; men and women who place principle over possessions; men and women who know their business and attend to it; who know it's not how long you live but how well; who will not lie and will not dodge their responsibilities; who are not afraid of speaking their mind; men and women who can look you in the eye; but above all, the world is searching for the men and women who can say "I love you" and mean it!

To my children and grandchildren I pray that I've taught you well. So often I try to address the question: "Have I completed my task? Did I do enough? Have I taught you everything you need to know?"

Have I taught you to count your blessings, to pause whenever you feel sorry for yourself, and to remember, this is the only day you will possess so live it to the fullest? Have I taught you to never abandon hope or give up on life? Life is a gift from God. As long as there is a bleep on the monitor screen, never give up.

Have I taught you to count it all joy, to avoid the mourner's bench, and to embrace all trials and tribulations? I could care less about your past and where you have been. I am only concerned with where you are headed.

Have I taught you to be color blind, to recognize the common humanity of the Creator in all people? You are not your brother's keeper—you are your brother's brother. There is only one blood that flows through the veins of mankind.

Have I taught you to listen to your spirit and rely on the goodness and guidance within? When in doubt lean on 1st Corinthians 13:13.

Have I taught you to realize your potential and become everything the Lord has called you to be? Have I taught you to move forward with love, courage, and confidence? Have I taught you to do your best and never skimp on the little things? Have I taught you to be the first to praise and the last to criticize? Have I taught you to never fear failure? Have I taught you the difference between falling in the mud and lying in it? Have I taught you to waste little time searching for peace and contentment because happiness lies within?

But, most important, have I taught you how to love? The worst feeling in life is not to have suffered. The worst feeling is to never have loved. As my Pastor's grandmother has said, "Love is not to be paid back, but to be passed on." If I have taught you well, your struggle has ended. God is smiling.

Love, peace, and joy,
Dorothy L. York

❖   ❖   ❖

November 4, 2001
Waterloo, IA

A MOTHER'S LOVE IS THE SWEETEST

Of all the fruit that life can offer, a mother's love is the sweetest. Unless you've been there you wouldn't understand. I know. Am I biased? I guess you could say so. But hear me out, you'll find truth in my words. A mother's love is a light that can never be extinguished; an eye that never shuts; an ear that never closes; and a heart that never grows cold. When it comes to love, we wrote the book. A mother will deal with any chore that confronts her, no matter how menial, no matter how difficult, regardless how trivial, as if her entrance into heaven depended on it being completed to the best of her ability. A mother uses love to lighten her load.

Just like my brothers and sisters, when I finished high school I married and began raising a family with the hopes of leaving the south in search of a better life. I was born and raised in Water Valley, Mississippi. You've probably never heard of Water Valley. It's a little town, population less than five thousand, not too far from Greenwood. There were fourteen of us—my mother, father, and twelve children—myself included. Daddy and Mama were farmers. As a matter of fact, everybody in Yalobusha County farmed, at least until times got tough.

In the early 1960s we packed up and left. Word traveled fast from family in Waterloo, Iowa, that the local John Deere plant was hiring. There, my husband would work until the day he retired while I played the traditional role: cooking, cleaning, washing, and tending to our seven children—four boys and three girls. When the children got older my husband left and I was forced to carve out a life on my own. I took a number of jobs cooking in cafeterias, hospitals, day care centers, and at our local airport. But this letter is not about me or what I've done or failed to do as a mother, grandmother, and even a great-grandmother. No, my letter is about love—a mother's undying love. In spite of it all.

I've raised seven wonderful children. The two oldest are doing quite well. My oldest son is a teacher in an alternative school in Chicago, and my oldest daughter has found her niche in corporate America. But my other five children—three boys and two girls, ages thirty-four to forty-four—now that's another story. At one time or another, each has been incarcerated, having been caught in a web of crime. Three at one time. One of my boys is sitting in prison serving two to five years as I write these words. It's the same old story—drugs, petty theft, and poor choices. But

I love all of them just the same. It doesn't matter that society has labeled them criminals, or that they have brought shame and disgrace to themselves and to their family; my heart goes out to each of them just the same. I refuse to see the human wreck that a life of crime has created. Instead, I choose to see the children that God has given me.

My mama always said, "When you lose something, replace it with something else." I guess what she was trying to say was to replace my bad habits with her honorable traits and qualities. I offer the same advice to my children. I specifically tell them: Take your eye off yourself and help someone who is coping with a difficult challenge. Stop going to those places that mean nothing but harm. Instead, go to church and set a positive example for our young folks. There's no telling how much good you could do if you would put your mind to it. I've told my children more than once: You need to make a decision. Are you going to watch life or live life? It's that simple. I pray they will begin to correct their ways and make the right choices. But if they don't, my love will always be there, unconditionally.

Whatever else you are obliged to neglect, never dismiss a mother's love. The time may come when you will stand by your mother's bedside during her final hour, and wish you had never taken her for granted. There is no other human love like a mother's love, which follows her child from the cradle to the grave, never once abandons, never forsakes, no matter how unfortunate, no matter how difficult the hour. No child of mine could ever fall so low as to sink beneath my reach. When society turns its back, when the prison door closes behind, when companions flee, when sympathy and mercy depart, when the world judges and then forgets, I will remember and love my child. I will sacrifice every comfort and surrender every pleasure to ensure my child's convenience. A father may turn his back, siblings may stop speaking, lifelong friends may depart, but a mother's love endures to the end. She uplifts him in the slums, she embraces her in the alley, she comforts her in the clinic, and steadies him before the judge. When nothing else is left, when push comes to shove, she is there through thick and thin. Hers is a love that never fails.

I don't need a medal nor special recognition.
My heart is full, and that is more than enough,
Flora Kelly

❖   ❖   ❖

August 12, 2002
Dartmouth, Nova Scotia, Canada

LOVE KNOWS NO COLOR (2)

It all started with a picture—a photo that my husband and I saw in the morning newspaper. Her little body seemed so restless in that stroller. I mean, how on earth could something be so precious? She had the smoothest light brown skin, deep dimples, and the sweetest angelic smile. Her tiny face was swallowed up by mounds of curly brown hair. In a word, she was perfect. As I stared at her picture our souls connected. Her eyes seemed to plead with me to take her home. The next day a co-worker mentioned that the two adults captured in that picture were really foster parents and that Sarah, the infant in the stroller, was up for adoption. Refusing to believe my ears, I questioned why anyone would want to give up something that beautiful. With her face fresh in our minds that evening, my husband and I discussed the possibility of adoption. Without much discussion it was a done deal. We would start the process first thing in the morning.

Navigating the maze of red tape and completing the endless streams of paperwork was exhausting. Grappling with the touchy subject of race was no walk in the park either. In a naive attempt to find a perfect fit,

case workers searched for an environment that was culturally conducive to
a child with Sarah's background. Never mind our outlook that asserts
bloodlines and birth certificates don't make a family—people do.
Though skin color was a major issue with the courts, it was and is nothing more than a footnote in our family. Though John and I are educated
and come from stable, middle-class families, we are both white. Sarah, if
you haven't guessed, is mixed: Her mother is white and her father, black.
The story goes that her parents were together for only a brief encounter
before their relationship soured. The product of that unlikely union was
a beautiful baby girl who would soon be given up for adoption. After
much anxiety we finally brought Sarah home, a week short of her first
birthday.

I say to anyone who asks, I have three children: two sons and a
daughter. From day one my little girl was an equal. There has never been
a single moment when we haven't loved Sarah to pieces. She had John
wrapped around her finger. Even as a youngster, this bright-eyed little girl
boasted such lovable qualities. Her smile and personality grabbed those
around her and held on tight. She was imaginative, friendly, and loving.
For example, she taught my father, her grandfather, how to hug and express affection for his children, which wasn't easy to do. To be honest, my
father was a very staid, reserved Scotsman with blood as blue as the At-
lantic. But whenever Sarah visited—which was often—this little bundle
of energy with the mischievous smile would shatter any and all barriers.
She would run into his arms and smother him with love and wet kisses.
Though the differences between my daughter and my father were real and
alive, nothing could trample their fragile connection.

I remember one day when she was eight, Sarah and I sat in the
women's locker room at our local Y. A woman dressing in a nearby stall
looked at me before looking at Sarah. Somewhat confused, she said,
"You don't look anything like your mother. You must favor your father."

"I do look like my mother," Sarah replied proudly, reaching for my
hand. After giving us the once over again the woman insisted, "No, you

don't. You must look like your Dad." Refusing to buckle under, Sarah shot back, "Yeah, but I look like my mom on the inside." Though Sarah was taught never to disrespect her elders, she would never be diminished or defined by the idle comments of another—intentional or not.

And did I mention that she is a natural-born athlete? Every sport she tried, she played with effortless grace. Though she had never touched a pair of skates in her life, Sarah began ice skating at two, mimicking moves she had seen on television. I was in awe of her skating prowess but not nearly as stunned when she began to ski five years later, motivating me to take up the sport at age forty. From there, ballet and soccer weren't far behind. Before it was said and done, even as a high school freshman, Sarah would leave her mark on the varsity soccer team.

But then, something snapped. Somewhat facetiously, I tell all who will listen that everything was fine until Sarah messed around and turned fourteen. Hers is a life that flies in the face of logic. Here is a child who was caring, well liked, and a model student who then became rebellious, openly defiant, discourteous, someone who refused to accept any type of authority. As a result, she moved from school to school, switching from public to private, then back to public before she was finally asked to leave. Furthermore, Sarah grew cold and distant, quick to speak her mind and express her African roots, regardless of time or place.

In order to keep the peace, John and I were willing to relax our grip. With regard to our household rules, we were willing to bend but we refused to break. But sooner or later everyone reaches a limit. Under no circumstances would we tolerate brushes with the law, filthy abusive language (you should've heard the garbage that came out of her mouth), or unsavory friends. I believe in my heart of hearts these were the malcontents that introduced her to drugs—and low self-esteem. We fought often, and even today, we both know what will raise the hair on each other's neck.

As one could fathom, we tried all the usual solutions: withholding privileges as well as enrolling her in a child guidance clinic and anger management classes. We even sent her to a child psychiatrist—any and every thing to get to the source of the problem. Unfortunately, these therapy and counseling sessions, not to mention expert opinions, left me with more questions than answers. I thought I knew what was happening to my child but I guess I was wrong. At seventeen, Sarah did agree to spend six weeks in a facility for troubled teens. Though she volunteered, during therapy sessions she told her counselors that I was a poor mother and was dealing drugs. No need to take issue, the counselors knew better. And then came the lowest point of my life: I didn't know if I was coming or going when I discovered that Sarah was prostituting. A few weeks later she dropped out of school altogether and moved, with the help of her pimp, to Toronto. I just cried into my hands.

Today, Sarah is twenty-five. In the past four years she has lost two babies. Miscarriages. One fetus had developed Monro's syndrome—the doctors indicated the cause may have been drug related—and had to be taken in the third trimester. I couldn't force myself to be there. I've been told that I wear my emotions. Instead, my husband spent his fiftieth birthday coaxing our daughter through this nightmare. Now, I'm not blaming anyone for the circumstances surrounding Sarah's life. I'm beyond that. However, if truth be told, I believe the cause of her anguish and aggression, her desperate desire to disconnect, just might be due to the fact that Sarah was rejected in utero. Not only did her birth mother not want her but it was the social worker who gave her the name "Sarah."

Though I see my daughter and granddaughter—more than a year ago she gave birth to a beautiful little girl—every now and then, I don't have the slightest idea what Sarah does for a living. And to be honest, I don't want to know. John and I had our child for seventeen wonderful years and we are grateful for the time we had together. We adored her and still do. There's nothing Sarah could do that will ever shatter our love. After all, she made me a grandmother. I realized long ago it makes little difference how troubling the moment or how hopeless the outlook. God's love will dissolve it all. Nevertheless, if I could write one letter to my daughter I'd share with her the words that were written on my heart nearly ten years ago:

I gave my all, every ounce of my being. I love you. My love bears all things, believes all things, hopes all things, and endures all things. It's all that I am, and all that I will be. It's what keeps me going. Faith makes all things possible, hope makes all things bright, and love makes all things easy. My love is a beacon that, hopefully, will one day guide your heart back home. But Sweetheart, I am only human. Because so many of our years were marked by your chaotic and abusive behavior directed at me and your father, the very people you depended upon for your survival, there's only so much I can do or take. I've wasted precious years and countless tears. Yes, I love you more than you will ever know. But I also love myself. Over the past few years I've been abused and bruised. My emotions have been drained dry. So this is the day that I am going to be made well. I've got to begin to take care of me. I refuse to be hurt any longer. You can't go to a dry well looking for water. Today, I desire to be made whole. Therefore . . .

Sometimes love means letting go,
Peggi Mackenzie-Young

Chapter Six

Wanted: A Man

What do you think it means to be a man? According to our black grand-mothers, being a man has little to do with how many women you seduce, children you father, or people you oppress. Manhood is about setting an example through your behavior, facing personal and collective problems honestly, and work-ing to alleviate them. Finally, manhood involves knowing the difference between right and wrong and refusing to substitute excuses and expediency for what is right. Too many of your peers believe that in the attempt to get over, anything goes. Well, it doesn't. The price paid for this attitude is far greater than if you would simply do what is right and just.

When it is all said and done, what matters most to a man? The affection of his wife and the understanding of his children. All else is of little consequence. If you claim to be a man, it is your job to forge the family, shoulder the burdens, make the first impression, and mentor young minds. It is your job to make happy the home, to nurture all the virtues, and provide direction and instruction that is good and true. It is your task to receive the infant as it enters the world as well as to comfort the aged as life trickles past. It is your job to minister to your neighbor, attending to him or her in sickness or grief, consoling him after he toils, and loving all when the heart is chilled. It is your responsibility to be a friend and a benefactor, and, in the church, a devout worshiper and an exemplary believer of the faith. It is your responsibil-ity to perform the possible and trust the Lord with the impossible. Others may enjoy here and now, but a godly man will also enjoy hereafter. Who does not love and admire the man who spends his days in kindness and mercy; who incites the selfish and indifferent to good actions; who lives his life through his family and faith? Irresponsibility and immaturity he despises, and they lessen at his bidding. Commitment and character he admires, and they grow in his presence. If life is art, here is a man who would surely be a masterpiece.

Woven through these letters you will come to understand that manhood also means marriage. Almost unanimously, these black women will admit they've never met a man who didn't want to be loved. But they have seldom met a man who didn't fear marriage. There's something about tying the knot—according to men—that's constricting, not enabling. Let them tell it, marriage is easier to understand for what it omits from their lives rather than what it makes possible within their lives. So to all male readers, fear not. There is a miracle in marriage, it is called transformation. Marriage is a transformation that is fixed in the law of our Creator: "It is not good for man to be alone" (Genesis 2:18). The man who remains single to the end of his days cannot help but to grow cynical and cold. By nature he may be as warmhearted, as full of generous impulses as any, but he has only himself to care for. He has never known the anticipation and excitement of two separate beings united into one flesh with all eyes fixed on the future. Not in a thousand years will he ever feel the sensation of two natures brought side by side, harmonizing in every respect. He has never shared life's extremes—the embarrassing moments, the dark temptations, the tragic failures, and the ecstatic joys—with someone so dear. He has never felt the necessity of striving to make happy the life of another. He has never known what it is to hold a woman's heart, full of tenderness, strength, and affection, looking to him for love and protection. He's never had a helpmate, a staff to lean upon in moments of trial and difficulty. Nor has he ever stepped confidently, thanks, in part, to the shadow of her wings. A man will never put forth all of his energies if he lacks something outside of himself to draw upon. He has never shown mutual respect and loyalty to one so dear. It's been said that love is blind. I disagree. Love is not blind. Love sees more, not less. However, because it sees more, it is willing to see less.

Therefore, a man who will not marry will never learn the lesson of patience taught only by tolerating the faults and habits of another. Nothing is more pitiful than to see a man bent with the weight of years who is homeless and has no friends attracted to him through marital ties. Courtships are sweet and dreamy but marriage preserves homes, blesses society, builds cities, fills churches, and adorns heaven itself. Wealth, talent, and ability can only carry our young boys so far. These assets alone will never take them to the gates of the highest form of their being: One man, one woman, one life. A man who is happily married is a success even if he has failed all else. A man, in every sense of the word. Always upright, guided by just principles, governed by the highest motives. To have and to hold, for richer or poorer, in good times and bad, and with his wife by his side. Here stands a true man.

If we could see a resurgence in this land of a man looking to his wife as his equal, his comfort, and his dearest friend; and a woman walking beside her husband—neither before nor behind him—as a companion, looking to him as the light and strength of her life, we would begin to strengthen all humanity.

Many erroneously counsel young boys not to expect too much from this divine institution. How dare they? Manhood depends more upon the commitment that marriage demands than any single act. The final rung on the ladder to manhood can only be found at the altar within the arms of holy matrimony. When men won't marry they not only break a promise, they relinquish any hope of reaching their highest calling: complete and full manhood.

What we desperately need today—in our homes and communities, in our classrooms and places of work—are men who are willing to stand. We need men who are willing to step up for principle; men who are honest as the day is long; men of decency, truth, and morality; men who respond to their conscience even when it is unpopular to do so. We need men who know there is something within that is not open for negotiation; that bribery cannot touch; that questionable friends cannot influence; and that money cannot buy. Something within that will not be sacrificed no matter the price. We need men who are willing to stand for virtue, for high standards in a world where indifference and indecency slowly rule the day. We need men who will not waver in the face of doubt; men who personify excellence; who hold a vision of what can be, and not what was. We need men who measure success by the quality of their relationships and not by their lifestyle. We need men who not only point the way to progress, but who will incite others to go forward; men who practice what they preach, and who will keep their homes intact for the sake of their children. We need men who will give themselves without reservation to a just and heavenly cause. We need men who are spirit-filled, love-abiding sons of the Most High. We need men who will teach their children about the God they serve. We need men who will kneel in prayer rather than stand in frustration. We need men!

August 31, 1998
West Covina, CA

LET THERE BE MEN

As the mother of one son and grandmother to three lovely young ladies,
I've always tried to serve as a mentor to our youth, especially to our young
boys. In this capacity I've raised funds to send middle-school males to
math and summer camps at California Polytechnical University in
Pomona, California. Whether fair or not, I chose to concentrate on black
males because of the label "endangered species" they've been forced to
wear. Towards this end, I recently composed the poem "Let There Be
Men." I believe in praising, empowering, and pampering the black male in
order to give him the PEP he needs to thrive and survive in our society. I
look at our young boys and I see two individuals: the man they are and the
man they ought to be. One day, God willing, these two men will meet.

Of all the words I could've written, these lie closest to my heart:

LET THERE BE MEN

Who walk in integrity
Who take responsibility for their families
Who look inward once in a while
Who can walk among the great and yet, not lose the common touch
Who treat their wives with respect at all times.

Let there be men . . .
Who train and nurture their children in a loving way
Who know how to count their blessings
Who know how to apologize and forgive
Who hold family devotions
Who value marriage and fidelity.

Let there be men . . .
Who are role models
Who respect and treat their bodies as temples
Who share with those less fortunate
Who dance with their wives every chance they get
Who know when to march and when to allow the parade to pass by.

Let there be men who know they've been chosen, and who have clothed themselves with kindness, humility, and love which binds us all together.

Let there be men . . .
Betty Ford

❖   ❖   ❖

July 11, 2000
Cincinnati, OH

BLESSED BOYS!

In 1956, my husband and I were blessed with our first son. A few years later, our second child was born, and was immediately followed by our third, both boys. Fifteen months later, believe it or not, another son blessed our world. Three years later, son number five made his entrance. And finally, our sixth child—you guessed it, a boy—rounded out our home. Who would have thought? Six sons! They were typical boys whom we love dearly. When they were given to us there were no instructions, no directions or manuals, and no connecting of the dots on how to raise them. We just prayed a lot! I truly believe when the Lord blessed us with these fine young men, He stayed around long enough to support and guide us. With His help, His blessings, His presence, they were raised in and with His love.

As they grew, my husband and I would take turns going to church, taking the older boys with us and keeping the infants home. Eventually, we were able to go as a family. We occupied an entire pew. I was so proud of my handsome men all polished and angelic looking on Sunday mornings. Space does not permit me to elaborate on all the wonderful, joyous, glorious, tearful, and sad moments we shared. However, I can tell you that as the result of His grace, each son matured into a good, educated, God-fearing, loving man. A mother's job, first and foremost, is to nurture and love her children: teaching and supplying them with the resources they need in their daily experiences. Along the way they will invariably acquire other tools and qualities, but the morals and love they receive in a home of love and spiritual guidance will always be ingrained in their hearts. I raised our children the way my mother raised me—with discipline and heaping helpings of love!

If I have any regrets, it would be the precious moments I missed in the lives of my children. There weren't enough hours in the day to cook, clean, wash, and iron, not to mention attend to their academic and after-school activities. Fortunately, as they grew older, everybody pitched in. Now, I stand back and watch as my sons help their wives the way their father helped me. This is a new era where both parents feel the need to work. Notice I said feel. My husband insisted I stay home with our children. He stated that he didn't want strangers raising his boys. He wanted to know on a daily basis where they were and what they were doing. He wanted to see their happy faces when he came home from work. We managed financially because we stuck to a budget and prioritized. We had everything we needed and some of the things we wanted.

My husband and I are fortunate. We have seen our sons become adults and fathers raising their own children, and true to form, God and love are obviously present. Moreover, our sons love each other and are not ashamed to express that love. Upon greeting each other there's always laughter, kisses, and warm embraces. I see the same emotions in my grandchildren, also. As the saying goes, "The apple doesn't fall far from the tree." My sons and grandsons will agree: The strength of a man isn't in the deep tone of his voice. It's in the gentle words he whispers. The strength of a man isn't in the weight he can lift. It's in the burdens he can carry. The strength of a man isn't in how hard he hits. It's in how tender he touches. The strength of a man isn't in how many women he's loved. It's in how true he can be to one woman.

Here's the lesson I hope to share: It isn't easy in today's world, but you must focus on your children—particularly, if they are boys—and make them the center of your attention. The greatest gift that we can of-fer our sons is to treat them with the respect, love, and reverence they rarely experience in today's world. Enjoy and cherish each moment. They grow up so quickly and then they're gone. As a mother, when you witness the finished product of your work, it's amazing, as well as a glorious trib-ute to the Almighty who made it possible. When God measures a man, He puts the tape around the heart and not the shoulders.

Love,
Sadie B. Gandy

⬥   ⬥   ⬥

August 3, 1998
Memphis, TN

THE TRUE MEASURE OF A MAN

What's wrong with children today? In a word: Adults. The true measure of a man can be found on the faces of his children.

Mennie Lou Tyus

November 23, 1999
Milwaukee, WI

FATHERHOOD

Men, move cautiously toward fatherhood. It is much easier to become a
father than to be one.

Mary Harris

❖   ❖   ❖

April 30, 2001
Nashville, TN

A FATHER IS HANDS-ON, AND THOSE
HANDS NEVER LET GO

After fourteen years and nearly one thousand miles, I was finally going to
meet my granddaughter. As my husband and I drove to the airport, a million questions raced through my mind. What is she like? What does she
like to eat? Is she a good student? Tracey. Now that's a pretty name. Is
she friendly, and does she wear those crazy clothes that you find on so
many young folks today? Does she have a sense of humor or is she the
serious type? Who does she favor, her mother or my son? Does she have
her father's eyes or nose or complexion or mannerisms? And, my Lord,
let's not forget the big question: How in the world is this child, my
granddaughter, going to feel when she meets me?

Does she feel joy in finding her father? Or grief for fourteen years
without kisses, hugs, or touches? Does she feel betrayal toward someone
who was supposed to love unconditionally and anger aimed at a man she
worshiped but never met? Does she feel gratitude for finally having the

chance to close the hole in her heart? Maybe she won't show up at all, afraid to meet her own flesh and blood. For the past few weeks before I met Tracey everything seemed to move so fast, too fast for me, all started by a phone call out of the blue: "Ms. Hamby," the voice on the end of the line said, "you may not know who I am but I'm the mother of a child your son fathered."

"Well," she continued, "his daughter is now fourteen years old and she has but one request: She wants to meet her father. It's been a while but I distinctly remember that his family lives in Nashville, is that true? And, you are his mother, aren't you?" The woman went on to say that as her daughter grew older, with each passing day every conversation became punctuated by the same simple question: "Where is my father?"

After I hung up the phone I could hardly catch my breath. I didn't have a daughter of my own, but I was thrilled to death for the opportunity to meet my granddaughter. I immediately called my son who by now was married. I told him of my conversation and his daughter's request. With his voice cracking on the phone, he agreed to fly from his California home and meet us in Nashville.

As a former teacher and guidance counselor, I knew this situation had to be handled with care. Fourteen years ago was an emotional period in my son's life. A time when he sought to find his own way. And whether a brief encounter or a prolonged romance with Tracey's mother, my granddaughter was the result of two people sharing their love. Nevertheless, the events of the day couldn't stop me from staring holes into anyone and everyone who could remotely be my grandchild as they walked off that plane. All we knew about Tracey was that she was small in stature, somewhat shy, and would look slightly more nervous than both her grandparents. And then the moment arrived. A few minutes seemed like an eternity before a beautiful, fair-skinned poised little lady strolled through the gate. What gave her away was not her looks but her walk. As soon as she made her appearance I blurted out to my husband, "With that walk, that's got to be Sonny's child!" I ran up to her and hugged her as if someone might snatch her away. I told myself that I wouldn't cry. Fat chance. I wept. My granddaughter wept. Come to think of it, everybody was crying. This was a moment to remember.

For the following six days our family tried to piece together life's puzzle. Tracey had drawn up a few questions she wanted to ask her father at the big moment: "Were you there at my birth? Did you get a chance to hold me? Did you ever wonder how I was doing? Or did you even care?" I ached for my granddaughter, and my son. Sometimes a child's needs and hurts are so deep they only respond to a grandmother's touch or prayers. Fortunately, there were more hugs and kisses. I stroked Tracey's hair. I touched every nick and scratch on her tiny arms. I had hoped that pictures and family would grow quick roots. "This is where your father was born. This is where he went to school. These are your cousins, and aunts and uncles." For nearly a week we went way back and came way forward.

Before we knew it, it was time for each of us to say our good-byes. Six days came and went. My granddaughter was about to board a plane for Detroit, and my son was catching his flight back to California. Time for one last embrace. Time to share a few more words that, if necessary, could last a lifetime. I told Tracey how blessed and honored I was to be her grandmother. I held her hand and told her to visit with me anytime. I shared that, regardless of the circumstances of her birth, she was special and that no insignificant person was ever born. We cannot go back and capture time lost, but we can make each day a bit more meaningful by giving and sharing our love. I told her about the strength of family and the power of reconciliation. A family means warmth, laughter, memories, happy occasions, and love. A family nurtures and cares for each other and, despite differences, accepts one another as they are.

Today, my granddaughter is twenty-four years old with two small ones of her own. Over the years we have grown closer and closer. We share each other's heart. As for her father? Well, that continues to be a work in progress. The connection has been made and they are beginning to bond. They care for each other deeply. Unfortunately, my granddaughter was forced to consider a question that no child should ask: "Where is my father?" Any man can father a child, but it takes commitment to see the job through. A father is hands-on, and those hands never let go. Not ever.

> Sometimes we don't realize the good we hold in our hands
> until it slips away,
> Mae Hamby

❖   ❖   ❖

June 25, 1998
Brooklyn, NY

BEING A MAN IS A RIGHT TO BE EARNED

I'm a single parent. I've raised six children—four girls and two boys—without an ounce of help. When my children were small I had little time for nonsense. I didn't tolerate smart mouths, filthy language, or dishonesty. All completed high school but one. Four attended college and, as of this writing, one daughter has graduated. Praise God. All are doing well except one son. In and out of jail since age eighteen, he is now thirty-one, and remains incarcerated. Go figure? As a child, he never listened. No matter how much I punished or spanked him, nothing seemed to work. He crossed that fine line between okay and going the wrong way, and wound up just like his so-called friends. If I told him once, I told him a thousand times: I can do a lot of things for you, but I can't make you a man.

I write this letter not as a grandmother, but as a keeper of the flame. Someone who deeply cares about our young men. Today, shaping our boys to become proud, productive, and responsible men can be quite a challenge. Until you raise a child of your own—particularly a male—you will never fully capture the meaning of my words. You will never know the joy beyond joy, the hope beyond hope that vibrates in the heart of a mother who is responsible for the welfare of her little boy. You will never know the sense of pride that motivates a person to become more than he is and to ensure that her child possesses the faith and fortitude necessary to make his way through this world. And you will never know the heartbreak of a mother who watches helplessly as her grown son, regardless of age, never matures, never fully develops, never moves beyond a certain stage whether emotionally or socially, never grasps the big picture, never takes his eye off of himself, never says "enough is enough," never leaves the boys at home, never carries his own weight, never rises to the occasion, never gets it together, and never becomes the man she had hoped and prayed he would be. Being a male is not enough. Being a man is a right to be earned and an honor to be cherished. I cannot tell you how to earn that right or how to deserve that honor, but I can tell you that a real man uses the word of God to guide his journey.

Marion E. Nixon

❖   ❖   ❖

January 2000
Decatur, GA

DO YOU CALL YOURSELF A MAN?

How do you tell your grandchild that her mother is dead? Senselessly gunned down in a fit of jealous rage. How do you respond to her sweet and innocent tears that wonder, "Where's my mommy? Is she ever coming home?" Sometimes I've wondered myself. I've given up the possibility of a solution long ago, but it's still good to talk. Deep in my heart I know Anasha's mother is at peace. I tell her that heaven is a place where there is no sadness, no tears, no anger, and no pain. We must trust that all is well.

For her first two years my granddaughter lived with her mother in New Jersey until that horrific day. Shot execution style by a former boyfriend for no apparent reason other than rage. Now I know what the Bible means when it says, "Therefore, take no thought regarding what shall you eat or what shall you wear" [Matthew 6:31]. You see, tomorrow has not been promised. I had my life planned out. These were the days of my life that I had waited for. Not only was I about to change careers but I was planning to leave New Jersey, moving more than three thousand miles away. But things changed, and I have adapted. In spite of the shattering circumstances surrounding our coming together, I wouldn't trade a single moment with my granddaughter for anything. Though she was two at the time, for the past seven years we've been in the process of rebuilding our lives. And during that process, we've been drawn closer together. We've learned to communicate with each other in a deeper, more meaningful way. We've learned not to rush through life as we talk to each other. We say what we really mean. We spend more time with one another. We show our appreciation for each other, and do not run through the day, taking it for granted that someone will always be around, because that might not be true.

But I'm concerned. What scares me the most is the question: What has happened to our men? I don't know what caused this young man to act as he did. Anasha routinely asks, "Grandma, why did he do it?" I'm sure it was nothing important. Just another senseless act because a young man lacked the strength to master his emotions. As far as I can remember, men have defined themselves by the shallow qualities of strength when an ounce of courage will do. Defining masculinity by strength makes you neither strong nor a man. In all honesty, it weakens your spirit. So do you call yourself a man? Then know your own strength. It takes strength to be firm but it takes courage to be gentle. It takes strength to stand guard but it takes courage to let your guard down. It takes strength to conquer but it takes courage to surrender. It takes strength to endure abuse but it takes courage to stop it. It takes strength to stand alone but it takes courage to lean on another. And it takes strength to love but it takes courage to be loved.

A man whose sole priority is to be a kind, loving father and provider—though his strength is never seen—is courageous in a way others could never match.

Jean Rhodes

❖   ❖   ❖

January 20, 2001
Decatur, GA

A REAL MAN

Women, we are the individuals who can really impact our men to be better husbands, fathers, and sons. I've always played an active role in shaping the character of my son and grandsons. If you ask my five grandsons who taught them how to catch a ball or shoot a jump-shot or explained the delicate details of the birds and the bees, I'm confident each will say, "Grand Mama."

Though my grandsons are quite young, at some point in their lives I've already shared with them the qualities necessary to become a real man. A real man isn't afraid to show affection. A real man honors his wife at all times. He holds her hand in public. A real man stays at home more and steps out less. He can be found at home tucking the children in at night. A real man takes care of his children by choice, not force, and, if circumstances necessitate, gladly pays their support, pays it on time, in the right amount, and with a little extra thrown in. A real man is stoic but able to express emotion. A real man is too proud to beg but not too proud to cry. He's not afraid to say "I'm sorry." A real man is financially stable and builds a future for his family. Doctor, lawyer, or ditchdigger is fine. The object here is not a man who can pay someone else's bills but one who can pay his own. A real man listens. He keeps his word and his temper. A real man is spiritually centered and he knows that a family that prays together, stays together. A real man knows when it is time to grow up and take care of business. Though temptation lies all around, a real man is guided by faithfulness and fidelity. He treats women as equals. A real man loves his wife and children because he loves his God. A real man is committed, responsible, and stands in a storm. A real man not only shows up, he shows out.

It is my desire that my grandsons be such a man,

Ann Harris

❖   ❖   ❖

December 21, 2001
Atlanta, GA

THE MAKING OF A MAN

Dear Khalil,

My first grandchild, son of my son. This letter is written to you in the year of our Lord 2001, the year in which your birth so richly blessed our lives. The moment you were born our hearts were full. I am so thankful to God for the gift of you. Yet no gift is complete unless it expresses the true nature of the giver. And, because I love you dearly, I wish to pass on words of wisdom that will aid in your daily struggles and provide a source of strength as you face life's frequent trials. I am often asked how I gained such knowledge. To be honest, not in school. Nor did I gather much from books that I read or lessons that I can barely remember. No, I was taught by life itself. I learned long ago, it's not what you eat but what you digest that makes you strong. It is not what you gain, but what you save that allows you to prosper. It is not what you preach, but what you practice that makes you wise. And, Lord knows as I've walked this path as a single parent, I've had plenty of practice.

Where should I start? There should be little question. First and foremost, develop a relationship with God Almighty, Creator of Heaven and Earth. Open your heart to Him and make Him the head of your life. Scripture tells us that God is everywhere and, where God is, you are. He is an almighty, all-loving, all-knowing, ever present Divine spirit. Acknowledge Him and thank Him for the blessings and gifts He has bestowed upon you.

Second, perhaps the greatest gift that God has given mankind is the power of free will. Utilize this power wisely. Life, at best, is only the blink of an eye between two eternities, and the key to your future can be found in the decisions that you will make. One poor choice can render a promising life useless. Whereas, the payoff for a prudent and sound decision is bountiful. Never forget, the cards that you are dealt are less important than the way you play your hand. In this regard choose your friends wisely, for you are judged by the company you keep. People may either enhance your life or impede it. The power of association can either lead you to the palace or to prison. Furthermore, choose your words wisely. Never allow petty spites to embitter your heart nor permit jealousy, animosity, or a silly quarrel to set you against your brother. Learn to control your emotions and settle any differences without violence. Be a man of character, beyond reproach, someone who can insert the name of the Lord into his conversation with ease. Remember the fruits of words and maintain a steady tongue.

Third, be yourself by living life on your own terms. For some reason or another there will be those who will find fault. These unfortunate few neither care for you or the manner in which you conduct your affairs. Never allow the opinion of another to determine your worth. Measuring yourself by the standards of another makes you neither happy nor a man.

Only you can create and define happiness. Whatever you are called to do, wherever you are called to go, enjoy the journey. Don't waste one day of precious life God has given you. Happiness won't come to you; you must go to it, and the place to begin is within.

Fourth, I encourage you to read and complete your education. Reading is a fundamental and crucial part of your development. An education, whether formal or not, will not only open the doors of opportunity but provide you with the keys to empowerment. To learn and discover is a privilege, whereas ignorance is a burden.

In closing, it is not enough that I desire you to be just, true, sincere, clean in body and spirit; that you tolerate your inequities; that you embrace the opportunity for riches because it will afford you the means of helping the poor; that you count your blessings and never abandon hope; that you meet and greet others with laughter on your lips and love in your heart; that you face every obstacle, meet any challenge, and stare down any difficulty unafraid and unabashed; that you dream lofty dreams, and as you dream, so shall you become; that you cherish all ideals and virtue; and that you climb the east side of your mountains— the side which sees the approach of the coming day, and not the passing night. But this letter would be empty if I failed to include one final gift.

As my thoughts shift to your father—my son—I wish to conclude with the poem that I gave to him when he was a young man seeking guidance and direction. To be honest, I had no idea if he ever read it. Years later as I was cleaning his room, stuffed in between the pages of his old high school notebook, I found a wrinkled sheet of paper. To my amazement, it was the same poem that I had given to him years before. As I told your father at the time, these words speak of who you are, and, perhaps more important, of who you may yet become. Though I have no idea where it came from, I pray you will keep this poem close to your heart. It is a token of how much you mean to me and the best road map I can provide on the making of a man.

THE MAN IN THE GLASS

When you get what you want in the struggle for self
and the world makes you king for a day,
just go to the mirror and look at yourself
and see what that man has to say.

For it isn't your father or mother or wife whose
judgment upon you must pass,
the fellow whose verdict counts most in your life
is the one staring back from the glass.

Some people may think you're a straight-shooting chum
and call you a wonderful guy,
but the man in the glass says you're only a bum
if you can't look him straight in the eye.

He's the fellow to please, never mind all the rest
for he's with you clear up to the end,
and you've passed the most dangerous difficult test
if the man in the glass is your friend.
You may fool the whole world down the pathway of life
and get pats on your back as you pass,
but your final reward will be heartaches and tears
if you cheated the man in the glass.

Anonymous

I give my word as well as my life,
Yolanda Daniels

June 3, 2000
Atlanta, GA

SUCCEEDING TOGETHER

It amazes me that some people can turn their heads and walk away from a disheartening situation. I've got to admit that I wish I could, too. If I have learned anything, I've learned that life, even at its furthest point, is way too short. In the blink of an eye or the beat of a heart, we come and we go. There's no time to run and hide. Flee from one set of circumstances, and sooner or later another challenge crops up and tracks you down. Running doesn't solve problems. Neither does wishful thinking. The only answer to your problems is to confront them head-on. Nearly twenty years ago, my children were not only fatherless, but nearly motherless as well. Today, however, through faith, determination, and hard work, my children and I have a new self-respect, and our lives feel whole. But getting there has been anything but easy.

In 1975, I was young, naive, and, having completed only the tenth grade, uneducated. After the death of my husband a few years later, I saw little hope in the future. My naivete had me believe that welfare was my only way out. Believe me, this is a part of my life that I am not proud of. I was taught that you make your own way, and that work is dignity and the foundation for a better life. For me, welfare was humiliating enough. But without gainful employment, each day I felt like a fly trapped in a web of despair. And then my situation grew from bad to worse.

I was on public assistance for a few months when the Department of Human Services inadvertently mailed me an extra check. Why I did it I'll never know. I promised myself that I would contact the proper authorities and make them aware of the oversight. But I didn't. Maybe I was tired of living hand-to-mouth or watching my children go without, but a day doesn't go by that I don't regret my actions. Like a fool, I cashed the check—less than $1,000. Months later, I was caught and sent to

Hartwick women's prison where I served eighteen months. The charge? Welfare fraud, but to be honest, I only deceived myself. I knew better. I could kick myself.

While in prison I soon realized there were other women in situations similar to mine. It's a commonly held belief that, once on public assistance, women—particularly black women—actually want to be on welfare. Nothing could be further from the truth. No one wants a handout. I counted the days, the hours, anything to the moment I would be released. Then I could begin to piece my life and my family back together. While incarcerated, I read my Bible and made use of the prison library. I decided to change my outlook and redirect my life.

As soon as I was released I gathered my children and searched for work. My daughter seemed well adjusted to having me back home. But my son? Well, that's another story. My time away had only meant trouble and, clearly, he had mixed feelings. He was floundering in high school—when he was going at all—not to mention running with a bad crowd. I tried my best to get through to him but, based on my past, he seemed to shut me out. I didn't press the issue. Within days, I found the perfect job. It utilized my skills, what few I had, and the pay wasn't bad. For the first time, I could see my way through. There was only one problem: I lacked a high school diploma. The personnel manager did everything he could, even bending the rules, but without that piece of paper his hands were tied. I had to complete my education. After twenty-five years, I decided to go back to school. I signed up for evening classes at my son's high school. For two years, I juggled work, home and family, and attended classes at night. From June to July my son and I took summer courses together to speed up the process. Once he saw my commitment, he buckled down and began to take care of his own business. As a single mother, I desperately wanted to be an inspiration to him—someone he could emulate and admire. Some folks said I got a late start. My reply: "So what?" Now what I get, I will work for and earn, and what I earn, I get to keep. A wise man said, "Judge me not for the deeds I have done, but for the life I have lived" [Titus 3:5–7]. I believe those words now more than ever.

And then, the day finally arrived. My son and I proudly marched together to receive our high school diplomas. He was seventeen, and I was forty-two. There wasn't a dry eye in the house. We've got so much ahead of us to learn, but that Friday in June was a good start. Now my goal is to ensure that my grandson has a fighting chance. I keep saying, he will be able to reach higher than I ever dreamed if he stands on my shoulders. So to him I conclude with the message I delivered at my baccalaureate service. I hope he will engrave my words on his heart:

I didn't raise you to be a statistic. You are different, and you've been chosen. I gave you life, but I cannot live it for you. I can teach you, but I can't make you learn. I can offer you advice, but I cannot accept it for you. I can show you right from wrong, but I cannot decide for you. I can offer my opinion about your friends, but I cannot choose them for you. I can advise you about sex, but I cannot keep you pure. I can inspire you to set lofty goals, but I cannot achieve them for you. I can pray for you, but I cannot make you walk with God.

Be the best of whatever you are. We all dream of great deeds, yet success lies not in accomplished works. Success is being the best that is in you. It is no disgrace to be a shoemaker, but it is a disgrace for a shoemaker to make bad shoes. Dream and aspire, but do not forsake the life you must lead. Make the most of what you've been given. Perhaps a trivial task is the one sure way of proving your mettle. Do the chore near at hand, and greater opportunities will come to your hand to be done.

The choice is yours. Take the first step and become a man among men. What the world needs are men—upright and God-like.

The meaning of life is to make a meaningful life,
Deborah William Thompson

January 2000
Baltimore, MD

I AM PROUD OF YOU

What should I tell you, my son? Should I say "I'm sorry?" Sorry because I have more questions than answers. What should I say? Should I tell you the best dollar spent is one that's earned? That fast money is nothing but trouble? Kids today have so much and want even more. I don't care what society suggests with its distorted views, you don't need everything; you only need what you can afford. Sometimes doing without can be good for the soul. If we could focus less on money and more on loving, we would all be better off.

What should I tell you? Should I tell you to never give in to peer pressure? Though I won't go into it here, one time you did fall prey to the crowd. And, brother, did you ever pay for your mistake! Do you remember my reaction? I pulled everything out of your bedroom but the box springs and mattress. "You stumble again," I warned, "and you'll be sleeping on the floor!" It was tough love but it seemed to work. I wasn't about to lose you to the streets.

Speaking of the streets, should I tell you how tired I've grown? Tired of all the crime, the violence, the killing, and the anger. Tired of the drugs. Tired of the shootings. Tired that so many of our sons have never learned to exercise patience and temper their feelings. And tired of the lack of respect, for each other as well as yourselves. Your cousin who grew up with you was senselessly murdered. He was so full of hope, so full of promise. Now, he is nothing but a memory. It still hurts to talk about it. Regarding our sons, mothers aren't any different. We share the same pain. We are tired of going to bed each night not knowing what tomorrow may bring.

Before I forget, I've got something else on my mind. Should I tell you how proud I am of you? Raising you as a single parent has not been easy.

But you trusted my judgment and always listened. Now, as you experience fatherhood firsthand, I can see that you're sensitive and hard working, and vow to support your son. My grandson is blessed. Boys need the examples of their fathers to follow. It can be difficult to be that example, but it can be done. Having you in the picture is so important. I smile when I think of you being the man that I knew you would one day become. I guess that says it all.

These are words that needed to be spoken,
Mary Murray

❖   ❖   ❖

April 2000
Atlanta, GA

LOVE, NOT DRUGS

I don't know where or when my son started using drugs. I do know that I was in denial when I found out. He was barely fifteen when he started hanging out with the wrong crowd. I couldn't believe that I was losing grip over my own child. Marijuana and alcohol eventually gave way to crack, and soon his cocaine habit was overtaken by heroin. It not only broke my heart to see my son in this condition but his addiction began to rip the seams of our home and my marriage. My husband and I were forced to mortgage darn near everything to pay for court costs and legal bills. That I could handle, but what put me over the top came the moment I discovered that my son was stealing from us and lying about it. I can deal with a thief but a liar, now that's a different story.

Toward the end of his short life he was caught stealing and sentenced to five years in prison. The night the police picked him up he was so high I doubted his guilt. He could barely stand. The commute between our

Atlanta home and the Morgan County correctional facility outside of Chattanooga was a nightmare. Me and my husband would drive up every month. I would look out the car window at the scenic view, catching tears in a Kleenex. "This can't be happening," I thought. "This has got to be a nightmare." But it wasn't. I would do what so many mothers who are caught in similar circumstances do: Blame themselves. Where was I? What was I doing? Where did I go wrong? Why didn't I intervene? I should've seen this coming.

As I walked through those prison gates I felt a familiar dread. Once inside his unit I would try to reason with him: "Aren't you tired of this life? Aren't you tired of living like an animal pinned in a cage?" I did my best to get my point across but to no avail. The toughest part of our visits was saying good-bye. Any soft words and silent tears were always shattered by the slamming of those jailhouse doors. As long as I live I will never forget that sound. I would cry all the way back home. When my son was released from prison his drug use escalated. By now he was a full-fledged junkie, shooting up in abandoned houses all over the city. It wasn't long before we discovered he had full-blown AIDS. I was scared stiff.

His last year of life we tried to make as comfortable and pain-free as possible. The cost of his care was not the issue. The quality was of primary importance. For nearly seven months he hung on and lived in a hospice, a program for the terminally ill. The care was professional and compassionate. But it started to dawn on me that I didn't want my son surrounded by strangers on his final journey, no matter how concerned or caring they were. I may trust someone else with my child's body, but not with his heart. I decided to take him home. For the few weeks we had together, I bandaged his wounds, warmed and cooled his aches and pains, and held him close. When a person is dying, there is an incredible urge to do something—anything—talk, cry, get a drink of water, run away, or stay. This was not the time to be judgmental. I listened without interrupting, and spoke without advising. I would stroke his hair and kiss his cheek. I told him how much I loved him.

Folks would ask, "Girl, aren't you afraid of catching the virus?"

I'd fire back "No! He is my son." Charlie would grip my hand so tightly as if it would keep him in this world forever. Through it all he never cried and never complained. His last words were, "Mama, I'm sorry I let you down."

Charlie died softly at home, in my arms, surrounded by his family. AIDS had gutted his immune system and wrecked his internal organs. He was forty-one and my firstborn. Dying is an art rarely done to perfection. Most of us are quite sloppy at it, very messy or bitter. But as Charlie went on his grand and fearless journey, he did so with a style and grace that left me shaking my head in astonishment and love. In many respects his passing was more heart healing than heartbreaking. His last day offers a perfect example on ancient wisdom about things that distort the order of life: Grief may take you away, but love and commitment send you back. I remember reading somewhere that we learn more from dying than we ever will from living. If that's the case, my son was an excellent teacher. At the time of his death I forgot all the bad things he did but I will never forget the way he died with dignity. Just thinking about him causes my eyes to water.

Mothers, when it comes to our children, especially our young men, you can put clothes on their back, food in their stomach, and a roof over their head. But if you haven't taught them to make the correct life choices, you haven't done a thing. I told Charlie more times than I can count, "Your worst day sober is better than your best day on drugs."

With all the love I can muster,
Myrtice Smith

April 6, 2000
Washington, DC

A LETTER TO MY GRANDSON WHO LOOKS FORWARD TO HIS WEDDING DAY

As you look forward to your wedding day and a lifetime of happiness, allow me to share my thoughts about this journey that I have learned from years of marital bliss. There are two ingredients that your marriage will need in abundance: love and hope. Marriage is a fragile flower that cannot survive where it is ignored or taken for granted. Marriage isn't for irresponsible people, nor is it for the immature. Marriage wasn't created for those who can't tell time, keep their word, call home, leave notes, or get in touch.

Love and hope are the beams that will hold your marriage together as well as the oil that will keep you and your wife from rubbing each other the wrong way. The love and hope which comes from the unity of two united into one flesh is a prelude to the divine communion of two into one spirit. Love is never fickle. Marriages that have love stand like rocks when the going gets tough. Love takes its vows seriously. "In sickness and in health, for richer and for poorer" means what it says. Love doesn't believe marriage is a turnstile, a stop on the road, or a phase in life. Love believes that a promise is a promise and that marriage is two people in love dedicating themselves to each other for the duration. Love is slow to anger and quick to praise. Sex is replaceable, love is not.

Love is too good to waste on the selfish. Love is a circle that is born of trust, beginning with yourself. The more trust you place in yourself, the more trust will be expressed in your marriage. Love means you give your marriage top priority. It means, if need be, you stand tall in the wind and rain, determined that the sun will eventually shine. Hope, on the other hand, will enable your marriage to endure. Hope focuses on the road ahead and not the trials of the past. Hope instills trust, even in the midst of failure. Hope looks at possibilities, not problems. I hope your marriage will last as long as you live. I hope that yours will be a happy home, one in which you can be proud. I hope that you and your spouse will not grow old before your time, either from worry or hard work. I hope that the years will bring you and your wife nothing but happiness. Your marriage is God ordained. It is my hope that our Lord will sustain it.

May these gifts of love and hope lift your heart,
A. J. Taylor

❖   ❖   ❖

March 1998
Morristown, NJ

BLESSED ARE THE HUSBAND AND WIFE

Marriage is beautiful and successful when you are willing to commit. Marriage must be the most important relationship in your life. If your marriage is good, you can overcome anything—adversity, economic hardship, and illness. On the other hand, if your relationship is poor, there's not enough power in the universe to fill the awful void. Nothing, absolutely nothing, is more important than your spouse. Blessed are the husband and wife who continue to be affectionate and considerate long after the wedding bells have stopped ringing. Blessed are the husband and wife who can sit on a porch and swing, never say a word, and then walk away feeling like it was the best conversation they ever had. Blessed are the husband and wife who've attained parenthood, for children are the heritage of the Lord. Blessed are the husband and wife who remember to thank God for their food before they partake of it. A good marriage holds so much joy, so many hopes, so many laughs, and an abundance of prayer. Build your marriage with love and thoughtfulness all the days of your life.

Rosie M. Howze

❖   ❖   ❖

April 29, 1999
Washington, DC

THE LOVE WE'VE LOST

I am a fifty-six-year-old born-again Christian and grandmother of nine. If given the opportunity to offer a single statement to our children I would address the so-called forbidden subject of sex.

Sooner or later, love is going to get you. It got me—or at least I thought it did. I was sixteen years old when my first child was born out of wedlock. I was nearly six months' pregnant before anyone knew I was even expecting. I was young, immature, and completely ill-equipped to handle the pressures of parenthood. Here I was given the task of nurturing another human being when I needed nurturing myself. My pregnancy was my little secret and I dared not tell a soul. But soon everything changed. My girlfriend down the street sensed that something wasn't quite right. One day, on the walk home from school she confronted me: "Girl, what's wrong with you?" she asked.

"What do you mean?" I replied.

"Don't play dumb," she snapped. "You know what I'm talking about. Are you pregnant?"

"No!" I fired back. "Why don't you mind your own business."

That evening, still unsatisfied, she and her mother asked me again— this time in front of my mother in our living room. Cornered and ashamed, I confessed. Her eyes moist with tears, I'll never forget the expression on my mother's face. She was distraught and she deserved better. "This wasn't supposed to happen to my daughter," she must have thought. Vowing to make amends, I stood tall against the wishes of those who suggested that I have an abortion. I knew I had made a mistake, but no shadow of immorality was about to be draped around my shoulders. Hands down, it was the best decision I ever made. Children, no matter where or when they enter, are our most precious resource. A year later, I returned to school with what little self-esteem I had, determined to graduate.

Many of us have been taught that sex is naughty and nasty, a dirty word. And though some of us may engage in it, we certainly are taught that we shouldn't be talking about it. I respectfully disagree. Holy Spirit has led me to a greater understanding and awareness of my sexuality, and has convinced me that it is both natural and healthy to embrace and celebrate this part of our being.

Today, between spoken and unspoken sexual messages, so many children come of age with conflicting feelings. Images of female sexuality ooze from every part of our culture—from the movies we watch, to the music we hear, to the clothes we wear. Our children, as well as many adults, receive their cues about lovemaking from what they've seen or heard. That usually amounts to a brief encounter at a bar, a few drinks, a quick kiss with lots of groping, then a mad dash to the bedroom. In this scenario, sex is reduced to self-fulfillment and uncontrollable lust. All too sadly, the destiny of any child who is thrown into the mix will be compromised by words and thoughts of "mistake," "inconvenience," and "abortion." Enough! This is not what the Lord intended.

When God created man and woman He did so with a distinct purpose in mind. Sex is God's way to let us mere mortals assist in the creative process. We, men and women, are given specific roles to play. For example, in accordance to His word man was created to be a giver: one who gives of himself, his time, his resources, his ability to provide for others, and his love. The woman, on the other hand, is a receiver. What she receives, she transforms. Not only does she receive every good and perfect gift, but she is humanity's secret source of strength. Though a man may wander and lose track, a woman keeps him fixed to a common goal and purpose. Whereas man looks forward to the final destination, the woman provides the compass, the midnight star, and the guiding light. She is a receiver, not to hoard but to use her blessings for the benefit of those in her midst. She receives love and, in turn, passes love on to others. If she is edified, she will, in turn, inspire and uplift others. And if her heart is broken, she is resilient. Watch how well she recovers.

Woman conceives the future that man tends to flee, and she feeds the children that man ignores. She transforms the raw power of male masculinity into love and sensitivity. She links man to specific children, and then rears those children into upstanding adults. Man may chase power and glory, but woman makes sure her male counterpart realizes the true meaning of life. When it comes to sex a man only needs a place, but a woman needs a reason. She is rare and sacred, fragile and special; something to be valued and treasured. She is priceless no matter where she may be found. What limited resources she is given, she can sustain and provide for many. Has it not been said, "One mother can care for many children, but many children cannot care for one mother?" It is her feminine wisdom that explains to her mate the golden rule of marriage: "Give and you will be given unto" [Luke 6:38]. She has a way of giving to all who seek her grace.

Hear me loud and clear. This is God's grand design, and these are roles and duties that can only be consummated under the covenant—the stamp and seal—of marriage. Not as lover, not as an acquaintance, not a blind date, not a boyfriend or girlfriend, not another pretty face, or a phone number in a little black book, but a spouse. No man can legally be the giver that God has called him to be until he first gives the woman his name in marriage. A woman, on the other hand, violates God's trust as well as her body, and forfeits her calling if she surrenders her virtue and honor to any man other than her husband.

And sex? Well, sex is the final act, the culmination of a single ongoing exercise of intimacy between husband and wife. An act that began with the hug and kiss good-bye in the morning. Which was followed up by taking out the trash and dropping her clothes off at the cleaners. The foreplay was continued by the phone call in the middle of the day to see how her day was going, to removing the dinner plates from the kitchen table, and helping the children with their homework. Because these two parties have been intimate all day, before they retire the final expression of adoration takes its natural course. How perfect and sweet. Only the Divine One could devise such a plan to bond two hearts. A love that arises from an allegiance to your spouse and to your God. When sex takes on this spiritual dimension, there's a sense of oneness with yourself, your mate, and the universe. This is the only way love can be equated with sex. Sex comes easy but love is hard to find. Sex may last only a few minutes, but love, respect, and affection will last a lifetime.

So to my grandchildren, to all children, before you get hot and bothered, before you start soaking in the latest music videos and rap lyrics, before you allow your young, fertile minds to be contaminated with pornography and the lure of illicit sex, please understand that saying yes to premarital sex is, in the same instant, blindly agreeing to its potential consequences: disease, possible pregnancy, emotional pain, and a violation of God's plan. Look at our world today. So many of us have no idea of our true purpose and the distinct roles of men and women. See the hell that we created by walking on the wrong side of God's law because we gave in to our own selfish needs and wants.

There is another way, a better way, a foundation that is the strongest link in an unending biological chain: First, the patience, love, and guidance of parents. Second, the inspiration and support of husband and wife. And third, the challenge and responsibility of rearing the next generation. We can make a difference in this world once we decide to go to the One who created us all, and invite Him into our hearts. I believe our children do not want to continue down this path to self-destruction but hope to regain every measure of their self-esteem and value, and to be delivered to the doorstep of their faith. It is their God-given destiny.

You carry the hopes of all those who care,
Elder Sharon T. Jones

❧   ❧   ❧

A CLOSING WORD OR TWO
ON WANTED: A MAN

April 1998
Newport News, VA

One of the greatest blessings of my life has been my marriage. My husband and I have been married for thirty-eight years. We were high school sweethearts. I've heard people say the key to a successful marriage is communication, respect, a little of this, a touch of that. Well, each of these qualities are needed. However, I know that a strong, healthy marriage is based upon God's word. "What God has joined together, let no man put asunder" [Matthew 19:6]. In other words, don't marry the person you think you can live with. Marry the individual you can't live without.

Mary L. Brown

March 31, 1999
Bryan, TX

I've always said, if I ever got married it would be for keeps. So, May 25th, my husband and I celebrated our forty-sixth wedding anniversary. Wedding vows take only a few minutes to say, but a lifetime to live.

Jewel B. Ross

❖ ❖ ❖

August 13, 1998
Houston, TX

Trust in a marriage is key. Regarding a pretty woman and honesty: If you don't look once, you're not a man. But if you look twice, you're not a man of God.

Cansada Smith

❖ ❖ ❖

October 1998
Lake Providence, LA

The Bible has a word to describe safe sex. It's called marriage.

Leola Whitlock

Chapter Seven

Go and Do
Likewise

s I reflect upon the words of these grandmothers, I have come to understand a crucial lesson they hope to convey: Every minute you drink from wells you did not dig, you are refreshed and fed by neighbors and caregivers you will never know.

You possess a marvelous power. This force alone, when used wisely, will enable average men and women to move beyond the limits of any human condition. Like the morning dew this power refreshes and revives. It flows from a good heart and looks beyond any need for recognition or approval. Here lies a quality that never opens but heals the wounds inflicted by anger, fate, or misfortune. A power that never incites but calms the troubled mind. Sadly, only a few even realize that an enormous ability lies within their grasp while the vast majority continue to pay a steep price in terms of stress and anxiety for their ignorance. Friends have been lost, doors have been closed, relationships have been damaged, and opportunities have vanished. This enormous gift gives us a consistent frame of reference, a model to follow when relating to others. Once you've unleashed this quality it will prove to be your greatest weapon—no one you meet can withstand its force. Your dress they may reject, your speech they may belittle, your background they may spurn, and your race they may despise. Yet this act of grace will win over the staunchest critic.

It is a principle that gave the world Martin Luther King, Jr., Mother Teresa, and Archbishop Desmond Tutu. At its highest, this virtue touches the wings of the divine. Here lies a power that transforms the skeptic and inspires the philanthropist in us all. No matter how tired or how tried, it blesses and curses not. When life passes by, whomever would be respected and beloved, whomever would be honored and remembered, must learn to harbor this trait. Though there may be differences of race and religion, this spiritual key is the Good

Samaritan of the heart. It is as wide as the world of suffering, deep as the heart of sorrow, and vast as the necessities of the needy. This power dreams of doctors who are more concerned with public health than private wealth. It envisions lawyers who are focused on justice rather than judgeship. It imagines the clergy who emphasize prophecy more so than profiteering. A conqueror is regarded with awe, the wise man commands our esteem, but it is the individual who embraces this key that wins our affection. It is the inner voice that demonstrates the greater good is the common good.

The deepest sense of happiness comes not from having or getting, but from giving. The fruits of success are available to all; however, our tongues will never enjoy its sweet nectar unless we share our good with others. Yes, charity begins at home, but it may and should go elsewhere. How sweet are its soothing words to the disconsolate. How consoling its tears of sympathy to the mourning. How fresh is its spirit of hope to the discouraged. How invigorating the company of its love to the oppressed. The poor and the needy should occupy a place in our heart. The sick and suffering should claim our attention. The sinful and wayward should awaken our deepest pity. The outcast and downtrodden should dwell in our thoughts. The fine art of serving and giving, to friends and strangers alike with no strings attached, is the best way of placing God's laws into everyday life. And, like anything else, the best place to start is where we stand.

I can't remember who sent it, but years ago a friend acknowledged a gift I had given her with a thank-you card that closed with a poem. The poem was simple but profound—there seemed to be a deep spiritual quality to the words. It is astonishing how such a short verse, the thoughts of some inspired unknown of a century or more ago, has endured, steadily increasing in influence and popularity. Since my first introduction to them, I have seen the author's words crop up over and over again in books, magazines, and newspapers. They are frequently quoted in plays and on radio and television. They've been proudly displayed on the walls of thousands of homes and offices, and have been translated into many different languages. No one knows who originally wrote them or said them. I've asked. No one knows when they were written or why they were written, or how they came to take such a firm hold on the hearts and minds of many. But take hold they did, impelling untold numbers to be gentler, kinder, and more considerate to friends and foe alike. They remain as fresh and vital as ever, a familiar little gem of inspiration:

You are writing a gospel, a chapter each day;
By the deeds you do, and by the words you say.
People may read what you write, whether faithful or true,
Just what is the gospel according to you?

Anonymous

The following letters are based on personal experiences and reflect the power of small acts to transform, to give new meaning, to bring peace and pleasure out of everyday events, even those that cause inconvenience, frustration, and pain. They are our black grandmothers' gospel.

◈   ◈   ◈

June 2000
West Orange, NJ

MAKE A CONTRIBUTION

Don't go through life as a consumer. Make a contribution. Find someone to help. Be your brother's keeper, no matter who your brother may be. If you've got a phone, call a neighbor. If you can find pen and paper, write a letter. If you've got two arms, lend a hand. If you've been given a conscience, show compassion. You've been given an enormous ability that lies within your grasp. As long as a heart beats in your chest, make a difference. No matter what your personal path to God, service is the first step on that path.

Christiana Lewis

April 2000
Birmingham, AL

SMALL ACTS OF KINDNESS

Raindrops may brighten flowers, but small acts of kindness brighten the world. Selfishness is the root of evil; kindness is the cure. Those who treat others as they wish to be treated stand closest to God.

Lula B. Daniel

❖ ❖ ❖

May 20, 2001
Atlanta, GA

GIVE A PIECE OF YOUR SPIRIT

I try my best to weave the spirit of giving into each relationship, whether among family, friends, acquaintances, or even strangers. One evening, a young man who was dating my daughter introduced his mother. This dear woman was so sweet, but upon first glance you could tell that life had thrown her a few curves. Her husband had left, forcing her to provide for her ten children. What little faith she had, in herself as well as in God, was definitely on trial. In the dead of winter she wore clothing so tattered and light that it made me think, "She must be freezing!" Before she and her son left my home, I was moved to retrieve one of the many overcoats that I had bought over the years and never wore, and drape it around her shoulders. With her voice cracking, she said she couldn't accept such a gift. But I insisted. My acts of kindness did not stop there. I noticed she needed shoes so I bought her a pair. With tears running down her cheeks she said that no one had ever shown her such interest.

One look at her face and I could tell her esteem was rising out of the ashes. It was then that I shared the words that have been a cornerstone in my life: "You don't need money to possess a generous spirit. You need only the desire to make a difference. We make a living by what we get, but we make a life by what we give."

Among the most treasured gifts you can give to another is a piece of your spirit. Here are a few simple ways in which you can make a difference in the life of someone else: Volunteer two hours per month at a homeless shelter. Send a flower or a fruit basket to someone who has made a difference in your life. Mentor a child. Spring for lunch at the office. Send a thank-you note. Call a long-lost friend. Prepare Sunday dinner for that little old lady down the street. Give up your seat on the bus. On the morning commute give your fellow driver the right of way. Send an anonymous gift. Take a stranger to church. Donate old clothing. Take a toy to a child in a cancer clinic. Prepare the resume of an unemployed friend. Offer a compliment. Help a child obtain a library card. Visit a nursing home. Help a neighbor with Spring cleaning. Donate a bag of groceries. Take a plant to the sick or shut in. Join Habitat for Humanity. Collect one month's worth of spare pocket change and donate to charity. Pay for the car behind you in a McDonald's drive-thru window. Everyone wants to do well but if we don't do good, doing well won't matter. Anyone can be an angel who touches the life of another.

Sometime it's best if your heart leads the way,
Gladys Hester

May 7, 2001
Baltimore, MD

LOVE THEM TO LIFE!

I am convinced that our actions on earth hold eternal life. It is up to each of us to determine whether our acts will increase the light in the world or add to the darkness. We are not saints, we are not heroes. In our hands we hold a single candle, sometimes barely bright enough to be seen. But to someone lost in the darkness, our tiny flame may be the road to safety and the path to salvation.

Several years ago as I sat in church I noticed a woman seated behind me in the back pew. She seemed uneasy. Her clothes were old and soiled, and somewhat out of place. At the conclusion of the service I approached her and introduced myself. "What's your name?" I asked.

"Anna," she whispered.

"Is this your first time visiting our church?" I asked.

"Not really," she replied. "I've walked past this church many a Sunday but today, the pull was too strong to ignore. Not really knowing why, I was led to come in. I guess I was just tired of being tired."

I learned that Anna was not only homeless but a recovering drug addict as well. At any other time, once her dilemma became known to me, I might have ended the conversation or simply placed a few dollars into her hand and gone about my business. But this was different. I felt the evidence of God's love. This time Spirit spoke to me and I offered to do more. In an instant I imagined there were times when people passed Anna on the street and thought, "What a bum. Why doesn't she get a job?" But it's not that simple. Few of us are so financially secure that we're not vulnerable to the same fate. Anna's weary face and outstretched hands could've been mine, or worse, those of my children.

Not only did I take Anna home with me that Sunday, but she stayed with me and my family for two months. I provided warm meals, a cozy bed, and a loving and safe environment. An admitted shop-a-holic, I even took Anna on a tour of my closet, giving her entire outfits—dresses, shoes, earrings—clothes that I knew I would never wear again. Like I tell my children, whenever you buy something, give something away because you don't need it. You've got more than enough. Anna, in return, kept the house spotless. Our brief arrangement proved to be just what the doctor ordered—for both of us. To those who know someone either homeless or addicted, I say, "Love them to life!" Eventually Anna entered a rehabilitation program and is coming along fine, supported by those who love her. I tell friends what I've done and they are filled with respect. They say, "I could never do that," as if I'm endowed with special powers. I'm not. I was drawn to make a difference, and I can't even say why, except for the words "But for the grace of God there go I."

We are not in this world alone,

Betty Wilson

❧   ❧   ❧

January 2000
Cincinnati, OH

A LETTER TO MY GRANDSON
TO SAY, "THANK YOU"

My Dear Grandson,

It's hard to believe the time that has passed since our last visit. It has been a joy to watch you grow and mature. I've had so many hopes and dreams for your future, and I am thrilled to see you chart your own course. Little did I know when you were small, not even walking or speaking, that you would play such a key role in bringing happiness to our family. You've filled our hearts with so many precious moments. For this, I am blessed, and I am deeply grateful.

However, it is important to remind ourselves of the hills that we climbed and the valleys that we faced which were eventually overcome. Challenges that brought major changes to our family. Do you remember how you felt when you discovered that your grandfather had to have his legs amputated? Do you remember the tense moments waiting to hear the doctor's diagnosis? Do you recall your tearful prayers? The promises set forth, the vows you made to the Lord if He would only spare your grandfather's legs? Perhaps you can't recall the details of those questions or even if they held answers. But I vividly remember the kindness, concern, and never ending love you exuded for your grandfather during his hour of need. Your tireless giving and thoughtful gestures became his lifeline to a normal life. Always by his side, it was heartwarming to see you dress him in the morning, fetch his medication, navigate his wheelchair through the neighborhood, and brighten his mood when you could've spent time with your friends or watched T.V. Little things, some would argue, but for a boy your age a major sacrifice nonetheless. Your unselfish dedication not only sped his recovery but proved to be the difference. What you gave your grandfather no one can measure. You supplied him with strength, love, and a reason to live. The doctor's prognosis may have been dim, but not your outlook. In a word, you are a caregiver.

It's hard to trace the trail of a single act of kindness. A gift from the heart possesses a life of its own. An act of compassion and caring can birth a lasting impact and touch those you will never meet or see. One tiny step from a devoted soul, insignificant as it may seem, can build a foundation that will not be shaken, cracked, or crumbled. These unselfish acts help relieve our fears, make believers of the doubtful, and soften the most hardened hearts. Simple courtesies like yours spell the difference in the life of another, and helps us realize that we can perform the impossible, change the future, and make life beautiful for those near and dear. We love you, and we feel blessed that you are such a significant part of our family. At eleven years old, you have met and conquered many challenges. You have learned that goodness precedes greatness. Continue to make a difference—just one tiny step at a time.

> The power to repair the world can be found
> within many small acts of kindness,
> Angela Davis

❖ ❖ ❖

June 10, 2000
Chattanooga, TN

ONE GOOD TURN DESERVES ANOTHER

I am a grandmother with two grandsons. My strength, fortitude, and courage to overcome life's obstacles come from my mother and grandmother who demonstrated the importance of love, kindness, and service to others—lessons that I have passed on to my son. There is no greater instruction than the example given by my mother and grandmother.

Growing up in segregated Birmingham, Alabama, my grandmother was convinced that education was the key to overcoming any obstacle that life placed in our way. To ensure that her children would not be denied opportunities she worked several jobs, not to mention washing and ironing clothes, in order to send my mother to nursing school. Thanks to Grandmother's help, my mother realized her dream. In the language of the day, Mother became a registered nurse, and, eventually Head nurse, serving the "colored floor" stationed in the basement of South Highland Hospital. She wore her position and title with pride.

In appreciation for my grandmother's sacrifice, my mother gratefully reached back to her mother, who only got as far as the fifth grade. By providing financial support, she encouraged Grandmother to return to school, where she received a high school diploma and, in time, became a nurse at age forty-eight. At the time, my mother was married with three of her eight children. It was Christian charity at its finest. My grandmother felt a tremendous spiritual calling to return to those less fortunate some measure of the blessings that had been bestowed upon her. My mother felt this need just as intensely, and she had been given so much more than even her mother. Her actions were guided by a desire to follow the Lord's purpose for her life, and she believed that every sacrifice she made was eventually returned to her in bountiful gifts.

This story has been played over and over in my family. Whenever I or my brothers or sisters complained about the discrimination or lack of opportunities, Mother reminded us of her achievement in the basement of that segregated Birmingham hospital. She explained that her salary was half of her white counterparts', and the conditions less than perfect; but with pride and dignity she overcame, and carried out her duties. Few complaints could be found after we realized how powerful this demonstration of courage, commitment, and kindness to others was evidenced in the lives of these two women.

So let us not grow weary while doing good—you may leave more behind than you will ever know. You can never tell when something you might say or do, just a little extra effort on your part, might go a long way toward helping another. The recipient of your gift will remember you and your actions for years to come. He or she may even pick up the baton of kindness and pass it along to someone in need.

Flush with pride,
Daphne Sloan

September 23, 2000
Swan Lake, MS

THERE'S ALWAYS ROOM AT THE INN

I come from a time and place where stories of the past help shape the future of those who follow. Sometimes stories are the most important example we can leave our children—stories that touch our hearts and teach us about life. The Spirit led me to tell mine, so here goes. This is the story of my life and journey. My schooling may have ended with the seventh grade but I've never had trouble with words.

I was born in Swan Lake, Mississippi, the heart of the Delta. Nothing really to speak of. Folks around here call it cotton and catfish country because that's all people ever did—pick cotton, and lure, clean, and cook catfish. Most people never heard of Swan Lake let alone know where it is. I can't say that I blame them. With less than five hundred residents, the town is so small it doesn't appear on many state maps. One of the larger cities, Greenwood, is nearly an hour away. As a child I remember trips there whenever our family had to buy more than just the essentials. Goodness gracious, we really thought we were something, going to Greenwood! Back in those days Greenwood was something to see. On the other hand, it's been said that Swan Lake can be found "thirty minutes from nowhere and the next town over from somewhere." In actuality it's seventy miles northwest of Kosciusko and thirty miles south of Ittabena. Sophisticated folks would mock, "Just take I-20 west out of Atlanta, turn left when you get to Tallahatchie County, and then steer towards the sky. You know you're getting close when you see signs pointing to Tutwiler and Glendora." Say what you want, but I'm proud to admit that Swan Lake is home. True, it's off the beaten path but here you earn everything you get. Folks are plainspoken, fiercely independent, and strong even in weakness, especially during adversity. In short, tough as any. Down here you make your own way. You do like everybody else: You work all day—and child, I mean all day—and make do with as little as possible. Make no mistake about it, from this tiny, dirt-road country town you can go anywhere in life that you want to go—providing you're willing to make the trip.

In Swan Lake I learned about family. Those who start loving you before you are born, and those you love even after they die. Family members who make your life worth living. It was here that I discovered the meaning of neighborly. Folks who may not be blood kin but treat you as their own. And, it was here that I met our Lord and began to realize a spirituality of daily life. Religion is a good thing to have. I have had mine since age twelve, mainly because I had parents who raised me up right. But I'm not talking about religion for its own sake. No, I mean seizing the time and seeing the Lord in everything you do—from going to school to reading the paper to sitting at the dinner table to meeting someone new. Life should be about finding God at every turn. All things considered, my outlook on life came from a family that loved me, neighbors that cared for me, and a faith that sustained me.

Nevertheless, living in such a closed and remote community does have its drawbacks, least of which is the lack of opportunity. Though once owned by the railroad, the land that my family settled upon was as fertile as any in the Delta. You didn't have to water it or till it; the cotton seemed to jump out of the ground. Though I was one of the fastest cotton pickers in the county, this surely was no life for my children. I was determined to see that my family would have an open door to success. So in the early 1940's, my husband and I packed our belongings, signed over our house and farmland to our next of kin, and moved to Kankakee, Illinois, a Chicago suburb. Once in Illinois I found two jobs. Good thing for me because I would need them both. My little ones weren't so little. I took an equivalency exam and earned a high school diploma and became a licensed practical nurse. Sadly, after twenty years of marriage my husband threw in the towel. He left right about the time my oldest child started college. After coming home from World War II he never got over his love affair with the bottle, and his drinking became too much to bear.

His life, however, was not without meaning or legacy. He left behind five wonderful children, each warm, intelligent, and loving. And so the best of who he is lives on in them. Initially, it was tough finding my way but everyone pitched in and we made do. For the next fifty years, I would earn my stripes as a mother and sole breadwinner.

By the time I reached my seventies I thought I would enjoy life as a doting grandmother, baking cookies and spoiling my great-grandchildren rotten. If only life had gone according to plan. Believe me, if you live long enough, life will throw you a curve or two. Several years ago I relocated to Atlanta, Georgia, where I lived with my oldest daughter. I had not been feeling up to par, and at her urging I visited a doctor who checked me out from head to toe. Well, there was no need for me to await test results that I already knew. Spirit told me. When the phone call finally came that morning I was concerned, but I was at peace. I knew deep in my bones that it was my doctor calling with the results of my exam. Now, I'm not going to lie to you, when he uttered the word "cancer," I did cry. After all, I was eighty-one and I knew this was the end of the line, and just like the body, sometimes the spirit gets tired, too. Nonetheless, I was at peace.

Unlike some folks, I never struggled with denial or asked "Why me?" Even after I saw the lab report with the words "breast cancer" written in black and white, I just closed my eyes and whispered, "Lord, if it's your will ..."

After the surgery I decided to go back home, back to Swan Lake. There, just like the ol' folks used to say, I waited on the Lord and the mailman. It's funny. When you're alone with your thoughts, and you know that your days are short, you begin to ask the big questions. Am I on the right path? Did I do my best? Did I do the job God placed me on earth to perform? I wondered if there was something that I wanted to pass on to my children and grandchildren. I remember hearing that the world only changes with one person at a time. If that's the case then, hopefully, I've done my part. I can recall all the times my daughters would bring someone home from college. Sometimes it was a roommate or a friend or just an acquaintance. Once they brought home a young girl who was evicted from her apartment and was living in her car. Neither of us, it seemed, had had a primrose path through life, but her story tore my heart out. Here was someone that needed a helping hand. And though we didn't have much, my children knew my response: "There's always room at the inn." As long as there's a bed, a couch, a blanket, or a floor, we were more than happy to help. You never look down your nose at anybody. You search for the humanity in every person, no matter how poor, and regardless of the circumstances.

If I could turn back the hands on the clock and rewrite the script of my life, I'd cut out the scene with the doctor's phone call that morning. I'd remove the cancer from my body and give myself a clean bill of health. But there's one part of the script I'd never change. It's the part about helping others and trying to make a difference.

Hopefully, the theme of my life is kindness: Give what you can. And if you have nothing, you can always pray. The kindness which comes to us, often unexpectedly, from those we know or even strangers we meet in passing; the kindness we show to others as we go about our lives; and the kindness of God, who provides all the blessings of this life, great and small, makes all the difference in the world.

When you share you always wind up with more,
Bessie Lee Hawkins Smith

❖   ❖   ❖

June 17, 2000
Chicago, IL

IT TAKES A VILLAGE TO RAISE A CHILD

It wouldn't feel right if I wasn't holding or caring for someone else's child. It's been that way as long as I can remember. After twenty-three years with the Chicago Board of Education and raising six children of my own, my life wouldn't be complete if I wasn't preparing formula, changing a diaper, or reading to an infant. My parents didn't raise their children alone—our entire community pitched in. In my childhood there were always another set of eyes watching or another pair of hands ready to help. Children need adults who love them, believe in them, and expect them to achieve.

A few years ago, a sweet, young girl from my neighborhood who was about to graduate from high school and was looking forward to college, got pregnant. Her family was devastated. Already disadvantaged, it broke my heart to see this young girl fall prey to premature parenthood. Filled with hurt and sorrow, she could see all her dreams and hopes for the future go out the window. Misty-eyed, I sat her down. I told her not to worry, that the Lord will make a way.

"Never give up on your dreams," I pleaded. "You can still complete your education. Just drop the baby off on the way to school; I'll care for him. When you get your degree, that will be repayment enough." Well, that was four years ago. Last May that young lady graduated with her class from Chicago State University.

Hey, we all make mistakes. Who am I to judge? My Bible says "Blessed are the merciful for they shall obtain mercy" [Matthew 5:7]. Most of us are not in dire straits but occasionally we get bumped into, rained on, or left out in the cold. These unfortunate circumstances may not matter much in the grand scheme of life, but at the time they can seem overwhelming. All any of us can do is to give of ourselves in service, whether it's to our family, to our work, or to those we meet. The greatest temptation in life is to settle for less than we can give, but at some point your heart will tell you what to do.

> By helping others carry their burden,
> you'll find the strength to carry your own,
> Rosie Hodges

June 17, 2000
Farmville, NC

THE QUICKEST WAY TO HEAVEN

I came up the hard way. I grew up in Farmville, North Carolina. Its name means just what it says: It was a farming town. My Daddy was a farmer. My grand Daddy was a farmer, and, as soon as he was free, his Daddy was a farmer. I grew up knowing that something about the land was special. I knew because my grandfather would work the farm every chance he got. Even in his fifties and sixties, during the hottest summer months, my father would get in the field and pull beans, corn, and tobacco. I quit school in the eighth grade to work right beside him. When I wasn't working on our farm, I worked as a domestic. Black folks didn't have much of a chance back then. But living on a farm, however, taught me valuable lessons, primarily, that you can find equal amounts of evidence to prove that people are either good or bad. So why not make them good?

I just turned eighty-one, and my farming days are long gone. Now, I like to read my Bible. Every morning, before my feet hit the floor, I read Psalms 97, 100, and 101. Folks ask me why these three scriptures are my favorite. I tell them, " 'Cause it seems as if the Lord is talking directly to me." I also like to crochet. It was my seventh-grade teacher who taught me, and I've been crocheting ever since. I crochet blankets, quilts, sweaters, socks—whatever I feel like—and I give them to whomever needs a lift. My favorite colors? Red, yellow, blue, and white. These colors seem to brighten everything up.

Folks will call me and say, "Miss Duncan, so and so is ill, can you knit him a blanket?" What gives me so much satisfaction is to crochet a blanket for the sick and elderly. The quilt warms their body as well as their spirit. It lets them know that somebody cares. While I'm there I like to offer up a little prayer. I call my quilts prayer blankets.

People say a great deal about eternal life. They say many things about heaven, streets of gold, and mansions on high, and such. Praise be, I've read and heard those stories all my life. But this I know for sure: We are taught to be grateful for the many blessings in our life. The least I can do is to give someone a blanket and a prayer. I firmly believe when I finally stand before my Lord and Savior, He won't ask me what type of car I drove. He will ask how many people I drove to church. He won't ask me how big was my house. He will ask how big was my heart. He won't ask me how many promotions did I receive on my job. He will ask what I did to promote others. And He won't ask me what type of neighborhood did I live in. He will ask how many neighbors did I serve. If I can show my neighbor these acts of love, this is the quickest way to heaven I know.

If I've done any good, I know who gets the glory,
Annie Mae Duncan

❖ ❖ ❖

June 6, 1999
Harlem, NY

NEVER DISCOUNT A SMALL ACT OF KINDNESS

Last year, I moved from Denver, Colorado—my home of thirty years—to New York City. Oh, how I cried. I stayed cooped up in my apartment for two solid months and refused to see a soul. The big city is not my cup of tea. I tell my daughters that New York is for young folks. It takes energy just to walk up the street, let alone go food shopping. And the cost of living? Well, never mind. We won't go into that. Let's just say it's a lot more than Denver. I hated to leave my friends, but I'm seventy now, and I wanted to be near my grandchildren. It's been a while since I had little ones, and they keep me on my toes. So what snapped me out of it? What got me back on track?

During the time of my move I began the practice of keeping a blessings journal. Every night before I retire I record each blessing received as well as the blessings that I have bestowed on others. As I grow older my thoughts and actions revolve around one simple question: "How can I incorporate God's spirit into my daily life?" My journal is the best way that I know how, and, to be honest, I was woefully behind. Like I tell my grandchildren, I'm not going to be here forever so it's important that I give flowers while people can still smell them. And you know what? The kindness that I offer need not be earth-shattering. But just think—what a better place our world would be, not only for me, but for my children, grandchildren, and for future generations, if each of us rendered a cup of kindness to another.

Refusing to be a prisoner any longer, I left my apartment determined to make a day of it. As I stood at a bus stop I encountered a young lady who seemed to be out of sorts. Trying not to notice, I caught her wiping an eye as I reached into my purse for change. Moments later, our bus arrived and we boarded together. As fate would have it, there were only two seats left. Trying not to notice, I glanced as she sat motionless, catching a tear or two. In an attempt to ease her pain, I placed my hand on her knee and gently whispered, "Whatever is troubling you, Darling, don't worry. I'm sure it will pass."

At that point the woman began to open up. Her eyes filled with tears, she forced a weak smile and a nod. She said that she was going through a difficult period in her life, and that she had just returned from North Carolina where she buried a niece. Since the funeral she began to struggle with her own mortality. "I know it's tough," I said, "to say good-bye to someone who's younger than you. But I've got the answer: You've just got to take it one day at a time."

She shook her head and sighed, "Honey, if you only knew how much

I needed to hear those words. I get the feeling the Lord has placed you into my life."

Moments later, my stop arrived. I told her to have a blessed day and I got off the bus. You know how something deep inside you lifts you up, and tells you that you're going to make it? That's how I felt. Why I struck up a conversation with that young lady, I'll never know. She didn't know me, and I certainly didn't know her. So what? It doesn't matter. What does matter is that our time on earth is limited, and we should be about the business of doing all the things we're supposed to do but have yet to do them. Giving words or concern and consideration to our brothers and sisters is a good place to start. Before I pulled out my journal and retired that night, I knew the most effective medicine for my self-pity was to lose myself in the service of others.

> As long as there is breath in my body I will do my part,
> Clara Villa Rosa

❖　　❖　　❖

May 11, 1999
Chicago, IL

SPEAKING OF KINDNESS, YOU CAN ALWAYS BE KIND TO YOURSELF

In 1987 I retired from my job as a surgical nurse at Provident Hospital in Chicago. I was one of the first blacks. I really liked my job but it was time to go. My mother, bless her soul, was getting up in years and she needed my care. After more than thirty years—thirty-two to be exact—I had seen it all: cataracts, radical mastectomies, gall bladders, hysterectomies, total knee and hip replacements, appendectomies. You name it, I've scrubbed for it. I've worked on cases that lasted more than five hours.

It didn't happen often but when it did, Lord knows I was so physically and emotionally drained that I had to find the strength just to sit down. Most of these procedures were pretty routine but I don't care how long you've been scrubbing in the O.R., you never get used to patching up some poor child who's just been brought in with gunshots or stab wounds, not knowing if he is going to pull through. When cases like these come in, you're taught not to get too attached but sometimes you can't help it. When will we learn? If folks only knew the toll that drugs and alcohol are taking on our children.

In my line of work you come to appreciate good health. I don't know how and I don't know when I began the conscious effort of taking care of me. What I do know is that I got started about fifteen years ago and my routine has never varied. I'm an early riser, always have been. Every morning at eight I'm either on my treadmill or in the park adjacent to my neighborhood, walking ten miles. Next comes the stationary bike for roughly ten minutes which is followed by fifteen to twenty push-ups, a set or two of sit-ups, and light stretching. I watch what I eat—plenty of chicken, fish, and fruit—and always eight glasses of water. I've never had high blood pressure or arthritis, and I rarely get sick. I've really been blessed. The fact that I've been given a healthy body is no ironclad guarantee that I will always be around to enjoy it. So why not take care of it? I shovel snow in the winter and mow my own lawn in the summer. I've even painted my house. My grandchildren say, "Grandma, I can't believe it! You're seventy-five years old and you run circles around me. Why, you don't even have a wrinkle on your face." Now, I don't know about all that but I'm the type of person who likes to stay active. It does a world of good and, besides, I like being kind to myself.

Love,
Mildred Whiney

April 29, 1999
Atlanta, GA

DELIGHT IN DOING GOOD

There's a power that you and I possess that forgives seventy times seven, and is rich in blessings. With this act of faith we can feed the hungry and clothe the naked, visit the sick and shut-in, drop a tear with the mourner, and embrace the orphan. This angel of mercy consists not in gifts but in generosity of the spirit. It is the inner voice that demonstrates the greater good is the common good. Here lies the heart of our spiritual walk: To extend, without price, a helping hand to those in need; to search for ways in which we may strengthen those who have stumbled along the way. For this reason, I beg of you. It is not enough to be good; we must be good for something. There can be no definition of a successful life that does not include service to others. It is only by giving that we leave a space for something new and rewarding to enter our lives.

Willie P. Hunt

❧   ❧   ❧

December 11, 1998
Hampton, VA

PASS IT ON

To my three sons and four grandchildren,

We can all look back to that one individual who took special pains to help us. In many cases, it was a parent, a family member, or a neighbor. Someone who refused to be satisfied with merely doing his or her job. I believe there is a lesson here for all of us: What we do is vital and each of us can make a difference. A thousand years from now I can't imagine that many of us will be remembered. But when others examine your life I hope that my teachings will not only provide direction but be a voice for that which is right and good.

I pray that I have taught you the power of giving: When you serve others first, you serve yourself best. Give to those whom you love, and give to those who love you. Give to the unfortunate. Give to a worthy cause. Give a smile to everyone you meet. Give a kind word and you will receive kindness in return. Give appreciation with an open heart and soon you will be appreciated. Give prayers for the saints and the sinners. You will be blessed more than you deserve. Give hope and new life to dreams and dreamers. Sad will be the day when you are content with your thoughts and not with your deeds. And since you're in a giving mood, be sure to give God the glory. Giving in the form of service is closer to the heart of God than any other act.

This vow, I pledge to uphold for the remainder of my life.

Have you had a kindness shown?
Pass it on;
'Twas not given for thee alone,
Pass it on;
Let it travel down the years,
Let it wipe another's tears,
'Til in heaven the deed appears—
Pass it on.

Henry Burton

Your presence has made my life richer and fuller,
Geraldine B. Clark

Chapter Eight

What Keeps Me Standing

mong the many great spiritual men and women in history we may find a few, or maybe just one or two, who speak the language of the heart and give us inspiration. These are our guides. They are not to be imitated, but are to be looked to for strength to help us live our lives just as authentically as they lived theirs. Within these pages I have found such guides, and I have good reason to be grateful and even better reason to listen attentively to what they have to say. In their own words, I have witnessed their legacy. It is a road map for the successful, as well as the suffering, to reach those places within the soul that give life meaning. Their legacy is one of life's golden gems: a compass in a sea of trials and constant struggles that gives other spirits direction. Hidden between the laughter and the tears is a life worth remembering.

The grandmothers in this book share a legacy that few will ever forget. It is a legacy that cannot be overstated. Their presence shines through all contradictions and marks a trail for humanity to follow. They may ask the impossible but they demand nothing of us that we cannot do for ourselves. Their voices are a mighty shout, as well as quiet whispers with clasped hands and heads bowed. Their natures are profoundly and decidedly Christian, yet irrefutably and fundamentally universal. Their hands are on our shoulders, guiding us along the slow and deliberate pathway home.

It's not the philosophies, the theories, the impassioned sermons that we embrace in our older years that cast the greatest influence. Rather, it is the code of ethics and grounded lessons that we learned at our grandmother's knee. It is the habits that she taught and the strength and courage that she expected that matter most. It is the memory of whispered prayers, of bedtime stories, and old-fashioned ideals forever cherished. It's her victorious attitude, her unique prescription for living, her celebration of the family, and her invocation to the young as well as her benediction to the old. It is her softer, more graceful path that makes life much more bearable. It is her touching, compelling affirmation to life: Things may happen around you and things may happen to you, but the only things that really count are the things that happen in you.

From where do our grandmothers draw their inspiration, and in turn inspire us? Prayer. This is the elixir her soul craves, the glue that holds her spirit together. Prayer is her password to heaven; her quickest way to glory. It is how she got over. Society says entertain your way out. Alcohol says drink your way out. Science says invent your way out. The military says fight your way out. Philosophy says think your way out. And politics says compromise your way out. But her Lord and Savior who counsels her through that still, small voice says, "Come to me, the author and finisher of your faith and together, let's pray our way out!" Prayer is her first and last order of business. It is the language of her heart, the center of a humble life.

Her home is scattered with biblical quotes and other writings. "I want to touch the hem of His garment every chance I get," Annie Gunn explains. On her nightstand you will find the words to her favorite hymn: "Precious Lord, take my hand, lead me on, help me stand." A get-well card from years past insists. "If it's to be, it's up to me." Then there's Langston Hughes's "Life for me ain't been no crystal stair," as well as a bit of Psalms, a bunch of Proverbs, some Isaiah, and a tinge of Ephesians. Her crusade is not so much the fervor of a come-lately Christian but the steady quest of a peaceful soul bent on one day meeting her Maker. Believe me, she has found God. Not the God we meet every Sunday in church or the one we kind of pray to, but the heavenly Father who keeps her standing in good times and in bad. The God who sits high and looks low; the All-Knowing, All-Seeing spirit she embraces for meaning in life. She is a tireless worker who insists that life's difficulties will never stop her from being whole. So for a portion of her day—every day—she reads her Bible and other inspirational writings which help her to validate, once and for all, who is the real power behind the throne.

October 3, 2000
Birmingham, AL

PRAYER TOUCHES THE HAND
THAT MOVES THE WORLD

Dear Lord,

Sometimes I get so caught up in the rapture and beauty of my prayers, I forget why I am praying. I realize my prayers need not be long-winded, righteous, or packed with emotion. They need only be heartfelt, and sometimes the shorter, the better. Not earnestness, but sincerity; not desire, but affection is the key to prayer. It's not how I speak them, only that You hear them. Prayer touches the hand that moves the world. Therefore, Father, I know You will hear my prayer.

I pray for those in need, the less fortunate. May we understand that homelessness can be a result of circumstance rather than a failure of character. May we come to realize that service to others provides more joy than vain pursuits. To give is to love. To withhold is to wither.

I pray for those who have lost interest in living. Those individuals whose minds are numb and who are frustrated because of past failures or because of the conditions in their homes and community. Lord, when You created Your people, You did not sift through rubble to do it. We were not meant to be poor, helpless, or to drift aimlessly through life. May we come to know that the path to our dreams always includes obstacles—sometimes, unfortunately, because we're the wrong race or color, and other times because difficulties always lie on the road to success.

Father, I pray for our children. I pray for those who were born too soon, too poor, too weak, and too troubled in an all too violent world. I've seen too many of our children overwhelmed with the daily struggle just to survive, growing up without any guidance or protection. Unable to cope, unable to handle life in hard places, destroying themselves with drugs, crime and violence. I pray for the children who no longer believe in themselves, walking around with their pants down to their hips, profanity on their lips, nothing in their head, and not knowing where they're going but getting there fast. You can't discipline them because they've never been taught. You can't encourage them because they've never been inspired. You can't hate them because they've never been loved. I pray for You to instill the Christian values in their souls that were a part of my childhood.

I pray for those in leadership positions. It is not easy to be principled when everyone around you shuns principle. It is not easy to embrace morality when those around you remain indifferent to immoral behavior. May our leaders fulfill their promises, pledges, and oaths of office. May we seek out and uplift men and women of integrity who are driven by sound, godly convictions.

Finally, I pray for humanity—one person at a time. Make us instruments of Your peace. Teach us to love and honor each other, and to accept our role, regardless how humble, no matter how great. One is the most powerful number in the universe: One song can inspire a broken heart; one word can encourage a doubting spirit; one sermon can save a life; one light can brighten a darkened path; one God blew breath into my lungs; one mother brought me into this world; one husband loves me in spite of my shortcomings; and one prayer can lift a troubled soul.

I bow my head in humility,
Addie Pugh

February 5, 2001
Baltimore, MD

LEAVE IT TO GOD

Prayer gives you the power to conquer your greatest problem. Can't seem to find your way? Leave it to God. Caught in a world of hurt? Leave it to God. Life doesn't go as planned? Leave it to God. No job, no savings, no nothing? Leave it to God. A loved one has gone astray? Leave it to God. Something is missing in your life? Leave it to God. Passed over for a promotion on your job? Leave it to God. Found a lump and the test results aren't back? Leave it to God. Don't know if you're coming or going? Leave it to God.

He doesn't give us His word to taunt and tease. Be still and praise His name. He will restore your soul.

Ferdine Barrett

❧   ❧   ❧

November 2, 1998
Wilmington, DE

THE PRESCRIPTION FOR SURVIVAL

When and where adversity strikes, here is the prescription for survival: For a bad case of the blues, take Psalms 27. For an empty purse, drink plenty of Malachi 3. If discouraged, rub on Isaiah 40. If people seem unkind, swallow Proverbs 17 and get plenty of rest. If you need a true picture of a Christian, Matthew 5 always works. When doubt comes upon you, try John 7:17 and call upon His name. When your faith needs stirring, rely on Hebrews 11. If you need a bit of assurance, Romans 8 usually does the trick. When life casts you down, apply some of Psalms 90. For rest and peace, get ahold of Matthew 11:25. And if all else fails, take ample doses of the Lord's Prayer. I promise, you will feel better than ever!

Betsy Brown

❖   ❖   ❖

October 11, 2000
Euclid, OH

Proverbs 3:5–6

Prayer: It gives you the courage to show up for life when life fails to show up for you. My favorite Bible verse? Proverbs 3:5–6. It's what keeps me standing!

Katie P. White

❖   ❖   ❖

April 20, 1998
Wichita, KS

LET US BE THANKFUL

Dear Heavenly Father,

As we busy ourselves to complete the tasks of the day, we must be mindful to take a moment to offer thanks for the many blessings that have been given us along the way. Each of us can find the world packed with heartache as we drift from one crisis to another, until a tiny miracle lifts our spirits.

So until that miracle arrives, let us not take for granted the food we eat nor the clothes we wear, and the friendships we've grown to cherish. Let us be thankful for the families we love and who, in turn, love us.

Father, thanks for keeping me around a bit longer. I am old enough to appreciate the young, and young enough to appreciate the old. I may be weak and small, and my voice smaller still, but I know that when I pray you will come and sit by me. Help us to keep alive in our hearts the words of the Psalmist who wrote: "Not to us, oh Lord, not to us, but to Thy name give glory" [Psalm 115:1].

Lord, help me to be patient so my children will learn patience. Help me to be faithful so my children will understand the power of faith, and help me to love so that my children will be loving. Most important, let us not take You for granted. We pray for wisdom and love to serve and glorify your name. Help us to flood our hearts with your spirit.

This I ask for in the name of Your Son,
Darnell Grubbs

❖   ❖   ❖

October 3, 2000
Birmingham, AL

PRAYER IS . . .

My Christian faith is the foundation on which I stand. It is my most important asset. What has guided, shaped, and inspired me over the course of my life is capable of doing the same for you. Think God-centered thoughts. Read your Bible and allow the word of God to nourish your soul. Get to know the Lord. Praise Him, love Him, talk to Him, share Him, walk with Him, and let Him guide your steps.

Remember how I taught you to pray? Prayer allows us to direct our lives in a positive and productive manner. Prayer is a lifeline for the living. In the darkest hour prayer finds a star. In times of greatest need, prayer is a helping hand. And, during moments of pain and sorrow, prayer is a soothing voice. If you have failed to reach a new spiritual high, if you are unable to withstand the forces of fear and doubt, if you are held in check by powers and principalities, it's time to renew your commitment to prayer. Prayer builds back what life has depleted. Prayer is not about vision but it will open your eyes. It is not important to understand how prayer works—only that it does. Let the word of God be your main course, entree, and dessert. Without a faith in our Lord and Savior, Jesus Christ, the universe is not only meaningless but unmanageable.

Kneeling keeps you in good standing,
Bertha Johnson

❧   ❧   ❧

January 4, 2002
Oklahoma City, OK

I MAY NOT KNOW WHAT THE FUTURE HOLDS BUT I CERTAINLY KNOW WHO HOLDS THE FUTURE

More than fifty years ago, I lost a piece of my heart. It stopped beating March 5th, 1946. There's a thousand ways tragedy can force its way into your life. You can lose a friend or a relative, a parent, a spouse, or even a sibling—take your pick. But nothing hits as hard as losing a child. It is then you are forced to cope with a grief the likes of which most of us will never know. I won't relive the details, but my baby was burned in a tragic house fire. With burns over seventy percent of her body, I realized that her struggle to live any longer was futile and it was time to say good-bye. Shirley hung on for nearly one month before her little heart gave out. I wasn't the only one who had trouble dealing with her death. I received letters and telegrams from across the state. Whomever knew me or my child felt the urge to share their thoughts and prayers. Why, her entire kindergarten class attended her funeral. She left the kind of hole in the lives of family and friends that you don't even think about patching.

From that moment, I learned not to take anything or anyone for granted. Shirley was only six years old, but smart as a whip. During her final days in the hospital she would say to the nurses, "My name is Shirley McCauley. I live at 2516 N. W. 10th Street, and I want to go home." She had long, wavy hair, a smooth brown complexion, and the softest green eyes. I swear, when I dressed her for church on Sunday morning, you could just eat her up. Everyone said she looked like a little doll. At the time, family and friends accused me of worshiping my children, that I was too attached and overprotective. I can't say that I wasn't. They warned me that if you hold on to something or someone too tight . . . Well, you know the rest of the story. Without question, 1946 was the toughest year of my life. Yet though I lost a daughter and my youngest sister as well, I did survive with a new testimony of faith.

For me, healing has come slow—*but it did come.* It wasn't too long ago that I could finally bear to look at Shirley's picture; I guess we all reach the point where we are too tired to cry. For years I thought a cloud this dark could not provide a silver lining, but if any good has come out of my loss it has been my ever-increasing faith. As doctors and nurses attended to my daughter and alarms beeped all around her, I knew God was there. I constantly remind my six children, fourteen grandchildren, and twenty-two great-grandchildren that nothing is promised. Every day, each moment, is uncertain so there's no need worrying about things that really don't matter, such as what you're going to wear, what you're going to eat, and where you're going to live. I'm here and you're here and that should be good enough. I've lived long enough to see many of my dreams come true. I've had a strong personal relationship with my Lord and Sav-

ior. My marriage to a wonderful man has been long and rewarding. Our
children and grandchildren are healthy and thriving. I've been blessed
with peace and happiness in so many ways. To say that God has provided
abundantly over the course of my life would be an understatement. As a
believer I know there's a God on whom I can depend. When we understand how weak we are, we grow strong by leaning on the Lord. And, like
those gone before me would say, "I may not know what the future holds
but I certainly know who holds the future."

So why did my baby die? The answers anyone gives will never satisfy
that question for me. But ask me why Shirley lived, if only for a brief
time, and I can tell you. She lived so God could give me the desire of my
heart. A child of my own flesh and blood. A child who sits in the company of angels and with her Lord and Redeemer. When I am escorted to
heaven, I will see her again and she will undoubtedly say, "Mama, when
you're led by God don't worry where you're going."

I'm all prayed up, and I'm not worried about a thing,
Ruby McCauley

❖   ❖   ❖

April 6, 1999
Bellflower, CA

A LITTLE FAITH IN A GREAT GOD

To My Grandchildren,

There is so much that can be written—so much has already been written.
More than ever, you'll find countless books which point out how to succeed in life and how to attract wealth—in short, how to be healthy,
happy, and wise. It would take a lifetime to read and apply all the advice

these books profess. But may I suggest a better way? Since the days of my childhood I have learned to include the Lord on the important matters in my life. Over time our walk has grown closer, and He helps me to improve. Regardless of the duties of the hour, you will do it better if you begin with prayer. Though I'm only of modest intelligence, this I know: God is still God. The same God that pulled us up from bondage, blew breath into my lungs, and allowed me to enjoy one more day, is still God—now, and for everlasting.

Read your Bible and lean on the living word. You don't need great faith. You need only a little faith in a great God.

Milla Jean Grayson

❧   ❧   ❧

February 10, 2001
Odenton, MD

SUNDAY SERVICE IS THE HIGHLIGHT OF MY WEEK

So why go to church? Or, better yet, is it possible to express your faith without attending church? Yes, you can. It's possible, but not probable. It would be similar to being a soldier without an army; a salesman without a customer; a band leader without a band; a bee without a hive; or a rose without a scent. I can think of several reasons why anyone should attend church.

One, church attendance is a great way to soothe the soul. It's a chance to rub away any bumps and bruises caused by the previous week, sort of a one-day revival for the soul. Two, regular church attendance builds character. My pastor teaches us to walk with integrity, to do what is right, to keep our word, and to never mistreat our brother or sister regardless of their race or creed. Three, with so many of our young men either dead or in jail, the church may be the only place where we can find positive, black male role models. It's sad, but true. I remember someone saying, "A child brought up in Sunday school is seldom brought up in court." And four, going to church allowed me to regain my sanity. Perhaps it can do the same for you. Let me explain.

Over the course of my life, I have seen the havoc that both dysfunction and abuse can wreak on a family. My father was an alcoholic, my ex-son-in-law is on drugs, and my estranged husband was a wife beater. One night, I can't even remember what precipitated our argument—maybe my husband had a bad day at work, or maybe he didn't like what I had cooked for dinner, or maybe it was something I said—but at any rate, it wasn't long before he unleashed all his fury. Before I knew it, he was trying his best to drive my head through the kitchen wall. It's a wonder I'm still here to talk about it. I left him shortly thereafter. The Lord not only lightened my load, but I know He saved my life.

Sunday service is the highlight of my week. Several years ago, I walked into church broken, battered, and bent, and now I am whole. So getting off my rusty-dusty on Sunday morning to go to church, with my grandchildren in hand, is no big deal. It is the least that I can do.

Rest in His promises, and rely on His strength,
Delores A. Tabb

❖   ❖   ❖

March 16, 1999
Houston, TX

NO ONE CAN STOP ME FROM PRAYING

My name is Leola Harrison Banks. I am ninety-six years old. I was born July 13, 1903. My grandmother was a slave. She was a beautiful half-

Cherokee Indian who lived on a plantation in Talladega, Alabama. She had one son by her husband, my grandfather, before she and her master moved away. My grandmother was deeply spiritual. She was blessed with the God-given gift of a midwife. She delivered her slave owner's children and had five children of her own by her master. Her half-white children were sent to school and eventually college while her black baby worked the fields. My grandfather could barely read or write.

Once slavery ended she moved her family to Texas, and lived with me and my mother. I loved to sit at her feet and listen as she shared her experiences: She always knew there was a Supreme Power, she told me. At night she would gather in the woods with other slaves and pray. They would place wash pots over their heads to muffle their voices. If they were caught praying for their deliverance they would be severely beaten—sometimes to death. They prayed for freedom and a better life, and they prayed to have their burdens lifted. When times were tough there was a Divine Spirit within that motivated them to pray.

I learned from my grandmother the strength of prayer. Ten years ago, God delivered me from Parkinson's disease, and now I teach others how to use the healing power of prayer. Just like my grandmother, no one can stop me from praying. I pray all the time—lying in bed, cleaning my house, and even while combing my hair I'm talking to my God. You can enslave me, and I'll still pray. You can beat me, chain me, and tie me to a tree, and I'll still pray. You can place a blindfold over my eyes, and I'll still pray. If I'm out of breath, I will whisper a prayer. You can even tape my mouth shut, and my little brain will think of a prayer! As a matter of fact, I'm praying right now: "The Lord is my light and my salvation; whom shall I fear?" [Psalm 27:1]. My prayers may not be prim and proper—I know my English may not be the best—but as long as my prayers are heartfelt and sincere, the Lord hears them just the same.

As long as you are able to pray, there is courage and hope,
Leola Harrison Banks

October 11, 2000
Lithonia, GA

A SPECIAL PRAYER FOR MY GRANDSON

Please accept my apology for taking so long to write. I have one grandson. His name is Elijah, named after the Biblical prophet. It is my daily prayer that Elijah become a manservant for God. I pray that the Lord will surround him with His angels, and shield and protect him from the principalities in dark places and the wickedness in high places.

I pray that those in charge of his education will be men and women of God who will instill in him sound, moral, and just principles. I pray that at an early age he will come to know his life's purpose and move boldly and courageously toward his destiny. I pray that Elijah will walk in the Word and that the Word will be a lamp unto his feet. I pray for my daughter, Elijah's mother, as she has been entrusted with this precious jewel. May God "do a new thing" in her. May she seek His guidance as she raises her son. I pray God will organize her thoughts and direct her actions, creating a woman that He can use.

Last but not least, I pray that my grandson will be surrounded by loving, caring family and friends who will protect him in an insecure and unstable world. May he move out with certainty and assurance, may he step forward with his head held high and never go begging for bread. May his doubts diminish and his confidence increase. This is my prayer.

He is the author and finisher of my faith,
Naomi W. Arnold

August 14, 1997
Atlanta, GA

HAVE I TAUGHT YOU HOW TO PRAY?

My heart is filled with gratitude for the opportunity to share what I have learned. I know from my experiences that ours could be a much happier world. Dozens shed tears for every one who smiles. Though our Creator has provided us with the tools necessary for success, too many have built lives of despair and sorrow. Perhaps my lone gift is to mark with words a trail that others may follow.

As a single parent who raised five children in an Atlanta housing project, I needed parenting skills based upon spiritual principles. The values of our children are shaped by the examples set forth by their parents and elders. Regardless of what went on in other homes, I used a portion of scripture to guide my children, always relying on the verse: "As for me and my home we will serve the Lord" [Joshua 24:15]. For example, each morning before the tasks of the day were set in motion, we held hands and engaged in a moment of prayer. A family united in prayer releases a power that sustains each member throughout the day. We may deny it and sometimes we even try to hide it, but prayer is a privilege whereby we turn our spirit over to a higher authority.

Plain and simple, I have sought my God and found Him. I have worshiped in churches and chapels. I have prayed at baptisms, graduations, weddings, and funerals. I've prayed at my job and even during rush-hour traffic. You name it, I've knelt there in silence. But my favorite place to pray was at my mother's knee. I can cook, clean, feed, educate, and discipline my children. But I haven't done a thing until I taught them how to pray.

Lay aside every weight and cast aside every burden,
Ruth P. Greene

September 7, 1999
Waco, TX

A PRAYER FOR A MIRACLE BABY

As I began to consider all that I wanted to say to my children and children's children, each time I looked at my granddaughter I knew I could not say enough. Let me explain.

My granddaughter was born five months premature. This little miracle from above barely weighed one pound and could fit neatly into the palm of your hand. When her mother and I saw her tiny, frail body we began to cry. To this day, I still cry. I shook my head and thought, "Lord, have mercy. How in the world is something so small and so fragile going to survive?" Before we had time to agonize over her problems, nurses snatched her away and placed her in the hospital's neonatal unit. It wasn't long before the unit chief approached me with a poker face and said, "Grandma, these babies can run into a lot of money. I don't see how this child is going to make it. What do you want us to do?"

I took his remarks to mean that he was in favor of pulling the plug and letting my granddaughter die a speedy, painless death. I replied the only way I knew how. I said, "Don't you worry about the cost. Let's pray!"

Right there, in the waiting room, me and my oldest daughter prayed, and prayed, and prayed. I whispered, "Lord, You've provided for the birds in the air as well as the fish in the sea. This is Your kingdom. Please save me grandchild." I prayed harder than I've ever prayed in my life. I had to trust that my prayers were being answered because her circumstances would get worse before they would get better. I don't know how and I don't know when but sometime during the first day, my granddaughter suffered a stroke. Forty-eight hours later, her brain hemorrhaged but she continued to fight. After all she had been through, the doctors couldn't believe she was still with us. I kept reciting Romans 8:28, "And we know that all things work together for good to those who love God, to those who are called according to His purpose." There were seven other infants in this unit, and she was the only black girl. We named her Victoria Gabrielle because we were expecting a victory! Soon a specialist was brought in and assigned to her case. He wasted little time informing us that, if Victoria lived, she would never walk, talk, or hear, and would probably be mentally retarded. Two days slowly turned into ten weeks and this little baby still held on. At this point I will never forget the specialist's reaction: "I've been in this business for a long time," he said. "I've worked on hundreds of difficult births but there's something about a black baby and its will to survive." Once his words sunk in I wasn't able to hold back my tears. She was the only infant in the unit to make it. I had mixed emotions. My heart went out to the other families but I was grateful that Victoria was given a chance. After four months of ups and downs, we finally brought her home.

Still plagued by medical problems, she was not out of the woods. Her muscles were weak but her spirit was strong. She didn't begin to verbally respond until fourteen months, and she began crawling even later. Physical therapists stretched and exercised her little limbs three times a week for nearly three years. Every part of her body began to make improvements except her legs. She continued to suffer painful spasms. At age two, to correct the problem, a team of surgeons moved a portion of the muscle behind her legs and placed it in front. Though she had to tolerate a body cast for six weeks, the procedure eventually gave her the ability to walk. While she had the cast on, Victoria would just scoot around the house on a skateboard as if nothing happened. To keep her spirits high I played gospel music all day long. Her favorite songs are "Fully Committed" and "God Is Truly Amazing." Nothing could be closer to the truth. After the surgery the doctors warned us that she would need at least another two years of therapy before she would be able to handle crutches on her own. But the Lord had other plans.

On the first day of school at Head Start, God fulfilled our dreams—

my four-year-old granddaughter with the big personality took her first steps unassisted, without a walker or a cane. She said, "Grandma, I'm going to walk into my school today," and she did! We had tears of joy. It was truly a miracle. And, as for those folks who said Victoria would never walk, talk, hear, or have a normal life—just look at her now. She's in the second grade, and at the top of her class!

The Christian walk is a real walk. You've got to rededicate yourself every day. When I look back over the past eight years it's so easy to question, "Why Victoria? She's so young, so innocent and precious." And then God answers in a big loud voice, "You want to trade places with somebody else?" No thanks. Despite the burdens, the ongoing therapy and endless doctor visits, not to mention hospital bills that have eclipsed $250,000, I have so much going for me: My faith, my family and friends, and my little miracle baby—God's personal victory! What more could I ask for?

No wonder we call Him Savior,
Shirley Eastland

❖   ❖   ❖

October 30, 2000
Decatur, GA

BUY A BIBLE AND USE IT

Pray and meditate on God's word. Of all the acts that you could perform that will lead to a successful and blessed life, prayer stands above the rest. There is a larger power that we are capable of touching, as well as a larger life that we are capable of living. Prayer binds you and I closer to our Maker. Buy a Bible and, by all means, use it! Read a chapter every day. It will give you a greater understanding and a purpose for living. It's better to invest fifteen dollars in a Bible now, than fifty dollars an hour for therapy later.

Sincerely,

Natalie J. Harrell

❖   ❖   ❖

November 30, 2000
Birmingham, AL

FOR THOSE WHO HAVE GONE BEFORE

Each of us has a road to hoe, everyone has a story to tell. No experience is all bad, no word is ever wasted. Perhaps what I have seen with these eyes and felt with this heart could allow you to make a difference in your life.

I was born and raised in a remote rural section of Alabama called Bradford. To be honest, Bradford wasn't even a town. It was a mining community—one of the last mining camps in the state. If you were big enough and strong enough, and could handle the work, the mines were the place for you. From sun-up to sun-down everybody, and I mean everybody—my father, grandfather, great-grandfather, and even my husband—worked in those mines digging for coal. Back then it was called "grown man's work." It seems like my father and grandfather had a pick in their hands the day they were born. Both had little education but a whole lot of determination. At the end of the day they would come home all dirty and dusty. And their hands, goodness gracious, were like shoe leather. I said, "Granddaddy, your hands are so rough!" He would smile and whisper, "Baby, when you meet a man and his hands are smooth, don't marry him, because he's no good. He's never worked." Go ask anyone—nothing was tougher or harder on the body than working endless hours in those mines.

I really enjoyed my childhood, especially the visits with my great-grandfather. Our times together were always filled with candy and treats for me and my twin brother, and stories. Though he was so kind and gentle, he was a living, breathing example of how cruel life can be. Once, as a little girl, I unexpectedly jumped on his back. He immediately winced in pain. I said, "Grandpa, are you okay?" Without saying a word he loosened his shirt, took my hand and rubbed it across his shoulders. I couldn't believe my eyes. His back was covered with scars. I asked him what happened. His voice quivered as he began to fiddle with his fingers. He said he had been whipped during slavery. I was so little, but I remember it quite clearly. I was either too young or too naive to cry but my mother, who looked on, couldn't hide her tears.

As I grew older I wanted to hear more of my great-grandfather's story. I tried to find out the day he was set free but no one could tell me. And, it wasn't bad enough that he couldn't read or write his own name, but he didn't know where or when he was born. It was like he didn't even exist. Imagine living your entire life and never celebrating a birthday? I was so sad. Years later, I was forced to think of him again. By then I was a young woman living in Birmingham with children of my own when tragedy struck: Four little black girls had been bombed during a Sunday church service. I tried not to get too emotional but my children knew them well. They were playmates.

But don't fret. This letter is not meant to be sad or gloomy or about how times have changed. My thoughts are about hope for the future. They are about prayer and the human heart. I've been blessed with a long and healthy life. Though my hands may not have dug for coal, they have cooked, cleaned, mopped, scrubbed, begged, and borrowed. They are old and worn with age. My travels haven't been easy, but the Lord has remained true. He has been with me every step of the way. I may have bent, but I've definitely not broken. I want to rest but I can't—not until my prayers are answered. I pray that you will understand and appreciate the burdens and hardships that my generation has endured. I pray that you will take full advantage of every opportunity that life affords. If not for yourself, then certainly for those who have gone before. Whenever you mistreat one another or fail to value the sanctity of life, you hurt more than yourself. Whenever you give in to the plague of drugs or alcohol and allow your morals to decline, you hurt more than yourself. Whenever you drop out of school and begin to drift through life, you hurt more than yourself. So many folks my age and older never had a chance, never had an opportunity. Over the course of my life I never earned more than five dollars a day working as a domestic. I pray that you will remember that the road that you walk has been cleared by those gone before. So if you don't feel like going to school, then complete your education for that poor woman down the street who struggled her entire life. If you don't feel like standing up and making a difference, then stand up for those who were forced to remain silent. If you can't muster the strength or courage to follow your dreams, then do it for the generations who never had the opportunity to see their dreams come true.

You are a miracle, and you can make miracles happen. You've got the power to dream amazing dreams. If not for yourself, then at least for those whose prayers have guided your future without you even knowing it. Something good has happened to you today. I pray that you have noticed.

Do your best and God will do the rest,
Minnie Player

February 2001
Oklahoma City, OK

IN MY GRANDSONS' NAMES

You may not realize it, but you probably know my two grandsons. Two little, handsome boys, with curly hair and bright smiles, always playing, and more than willing to plant a kiss or give a tight hug. Everyone, and I mean everyone, knew them and loved them. They were two of the youngest victims pulled from the ruins of the Murrah Building in Oklahoma City. Aaron was five, and his younger brother, Elijah, was two when they perished with many of their classmates in the day care center. The image of the boys all primped up in their Sunday best, holding hands during a family gathering has been broadcast around the world. Aaron was the man of the house. Even though he had outgrown Barney, the purple dinosaur, he'd watch show after show just to pacify his little brother. Elijah, on the other hand, had a mind of his own. Whatever he wanted to do, regardless of the consequences, he did it.

My, how they loved to have their picture taken. Well, that snapshot has been etched into my mind, and though I try not to relive that day, my memory holds another picture just as vivid.

It was a beautiful April morning. The sun was shining, birds were singing, and spring was in full bloom. I had custody of the boys since the youngest was three months old. My son and daughter-in-law were having problems and it was felt by all that it would be in the boys' best interest if they lived with me. Ironically, I debated whether to go to work at all that day. The night before, I tossed and turned and couldn't sleep a wink. I got up twice to check on the children. I threw an extra blanket on Aaron and put Elijah in bed with me. I tried not to disturb them because they weren't the easiest things to jump-start in the morning. A few hours later, the six-thirty alarm launched us into our daily routine. By the time I kissed the boys good-bye at the day care and reached my office two and a half blocks away, I began to feel better. But then it happened.

I was in an elevator when I heard a huge thud. In those first hazy moments I thought the main computer had blown up. Within seconds, a voice behind me said that our building had to be evacuated. With my morning coffee in hand I, as well as a stream of co-workers, sprinted across the street. When I looked up and saw the sky covered with thick black smoke, my thoughts turned to my apartment building. I prayed it wasn't on fire. As security continued to hustle people away from the scene it became increasingly clear that a massive explosion occurred just to the north, at the federal building, and that it was far worse than anyone knew.

As dozens of us ran to the Murrah Building I searched for the day care center. It wasn't there. I tried desperately to force myself closer and closer only to be restrained by a police officer. I remember screaming at him, "But you don't understand, I've got to get my babies out." In the midst of chaos, I joined the parade of people wandering in disbelief. The odor of sulphur was so strong. I watched in horror as bloodied victims ran out from the federal building trying to get away. Others emerged from the building covered with cuts, their clothes literally burned off their back. Several cars parked near the scene were melted together. There was glass and debris all over the place.

Aaron and Elijah's father was living in Atlanta at the time. He overheard a conversation that someone had bombed the federal building in Oklahoma City. When he couldn't reach anyone by phone, he ran home to catch the events on TV. Within hours he caught a bus to Oklahoma arriving the next day. Once there, he caught a ride to the bomb site where he walked up and down the street, hours on end, holding pictures of his children.

For three days I raced from hospital to hospital, church to church, flipping through lists of survivors in search of hopeful news. Praying without ceasing, hoping beyond hope. I was sure my boys were alive. I knew they were probably injured, but deep in my heart I knew they were alive. Finally, on Saturday night, I was told that my prayers would not be answered. The bodies of Aaron and Elijah had been found. Words could not describe my feelings.

Well, five years have gone by but I miss being Aaron and Elijah's grandmother. My heart still aches. On the first day of school this year, I watched silently as the children were going back, and my grandsons were not among them. I felt so sorry for my son, Aaron and Elijah's father. For months he did nothing but cry like a baby. He would often ask, "Mama, do you think my boys knew how much I loved them?" We both cried. The world is not supposed to work this way. Parents are not supposed to bury their children, and that's where the challenge lies. I don't think anybody who loses a child ever gets over it. I just looked him in the eye and said, "Sweetheart, we are in this together for the rest of our lives. It can't get any worse, we can only make the best of it if we so choose."

That bomb did more than rip a building apart, it tore a hole in my soul. Though my life will never be the same, I am pleased to say I've begun to patch it together. After six years of looking back, I am ready to begin letting go. Therapy, family and friends, and my ongoing dialogue with God have helped. It takes courage to believe that new life is possible when all around you are signs of destruction. It angers me to hear people tell families of the bombing victims to get on with their lives. I'm concerned with what life they want us to get on with. Answers to the senseless shattering of lives do not come easy. Five years ago a counselor suggested that I write a letter to God telling him that I forgive him. I couldn't make myself do it. Why? Because I was filled with too much hurt and too much anger. I screamed at God and cursed His holy name. I fell into a black hole of rage, revenge, and sorrow. But today is a different story. I've grown to realize that God hurts just like I hurt. Sometimes angels cry, too. The anger that I felt is still there but I will not be consumed by it. The need to forgive may be as strong as the need to be forgiven. I will not be paralyzed by death and destruction, and hatred and anger will not have the last word in my life. The last word belongs to the One whose caring face is always turned towards me no matter how much adversity I may encounter.

So today, let us be a witness. Hold your loved ones a little bit longer. Embrace those nearest to your heart a little bit tighter. Give to someone in need more gladly, and live your life more prayerfully. Promise me.

Do this for me in my grandsons' names and in His holy name,

Jannie Coverdale

❧   ❧   ❧

May 2000
Indianapolis, IN

"IT WON'T BE YOUR TEARS THAT
MOVE THE HAND OF GOD.
IT WILL BE YOUR FAITH!"

I could not write this letter without saying that life has so much to offer. Yet, as each of you forge your own way, allow God's grace to guide and direct your every step. Trust me. I am a living testament to God's sustaining grace. His favor and spirit have been the abiding factor in my life.

Nearly six years ago—at the prodding of my three sons—I was bitten by the bug to continue my education and obtain something I dearly wanted: A college degree. My family assured me that, if anybody could accomplish such a lofty goal, I could. Imagine that! Me, a grandmother in her late forties sitting among and competing against students half my age who were equally, if not more, capable, talented, and driven. Just the thought of it engulfed me in fear and doubt. From the moment I received my acceptance letter, I tackled my studies with enthusiasm and inquisition. For six long years, I managed to fit a number of activities into an overcrowded schedule: working an eight-hour shift at a bank before marching off to school for evening classes that lasted until 10 p.m., barely seeing and talking to my family in between. By day's end, dragging and bone tired, I would return home where I would feed and tend to my husband, your grandfather. Many times I heated meals that had been prepared the previous weekend. Each night, it seemed my books became my pillow as I studied until the wee hours of the morning. And during finals, sleep was an afterthought. With no end in sight, my fortitude would be tested again and again. Unfortunately, I began to listen to the negative thinking of others who asked, why at my age would I choose to go back to school? After all, what good would it do?

There were days when I cried a river of tears as I walked into the classroom, literally drying my eyes with my notes. Though I never questioned God, more than once I asked, "How much longer?" During these difficult moments your grandfather was so supportive. It was his words of encouragement that lifted my spirits. "It won't be your tears that move the hand of God," he instructed. "It will be your faith! I'll let you enjoy your pity party for twenty minutes, then you've got to get back to work." Well, it's been six long years since I started walking down this road and I can now see the light at the end of the tunnel. With my course work nearly completed, next summer I'm inviting you, my grandchildren, to join me as I march across the stage at Indiana Wesleyan University and receive my degree. And, with a 3.9 grade point average to boot! Isn't it amazing? You never know what you're made of until you take on a challenge. The hard-fought battles, the goals won with sacrifice, are the treasures of life that really matter.

As I close my letter, I say to each of you, live life to the fullest. Make every day count. As you do, keep Christ before you in all that you do. Serve Him and make Him an integral part of your life. Through my example, I hope you come to realize that the road to success is paved with bricks of failure. Though everyone fails in some form or fashion, you need not fear failure. Besides, if you knew who walks next to you when you face life's most difficult moments, you would never know the concept of fear.

My spirit and love will be with you every day of your life,
Jeri Shipp

A FEW CLOSING WORDS ON
WHAT KEEPS ME STANDING

July 31, 1997
Atlanta, GA

You are in this world to make it better, to lift it up to higher levels of love, to make each heart and home brighter, happier, and fuller. You must live life as if the Lord were looking over your shoulder.

Sarah A. Reed

❖   ❖   ❖

March 13, 1998
Houston, TX

Times of prayer are times of growth. Prayer is believing, not begging. Pray, believing your prayers will be answered. Relax and wait in peace for the results. Your prayers must mean something to you if they are to mean anything to God.

Ursena N. Coleman

July 27, 1999
Dothan, AL

Don't ask your children if they would like to go to church. Take them!

Delories Miley

March 17, 1998
Shelbyville, TN

My oldest grandson is a graduate student. One day he was feeling quite
discouraged. He sent me an e-mail—yes, that's right, I'm a modern
granny—I own a computer. He said he prays but it seems as if his prayers
go unanswered. I told him that God answers all prayers. Not always "yes"
and not in our time. We must be patient. I told my grandson to do everything he could and to leave the rest to God. God knows what we can handle. My grandson e-mailed me again and said I made him feel better.

Prayer is God's first and last order of business,
Gladys Young Flack

❖   ❖   ❖

December 1998
Hampton, VA

If you've got to tell people you're Christ-like, perhaps you're not as
Christ-like as you think.

Sarah Stewart

❖   ❖   ❖

August 5, 1997
Columbus, GA

On that fateful day when I finally meet my Maker, He will undoubtedly
ask, Who did I help, and who did I bring with me?

Harriet Chinn

October 16, 1997
Pearl River, LA

The Lord is watching, so give Him a good show!

Emma Jean Johnson

❖   ❖   ❖

January 9, 1998
Bernice, LA

If you wait on the Lord, time is never lost.

Willie M. Dismuke

Afterword

As I read and fully digested every word contained in these letters, I began to sense a deeper appreciation for all that has been done on my behalf. Some passages caused a tear to appear. More than once I found myself evaluating my own life, questioning my values and beliefs. Always in the thick of it, never shying away from the truth, these women pushed open doors that should have never been closed. I realized that throughout my personal triumphs, in every good and great achievement, these black grandmothers have been my boldest cheerleaders, seated somewhere in the back, cheering louder and smiling wider than anyone else. Their words and wisdom are so gentle, and yet so powerful. They write as if they had special authority from God. Come to think of it, they probably do. It was their shoulder that we cried on, their lap that we prayed on, their arms that held us, and it is their values that continue to keep us rooted.

It wasn't long before I imagined that their letters, collectively, should come with a word of warning: This message could end your life! And, rightfully so, it should!

The words written on these pages should end a life of failure and frustration. An honest look at the troubles we've created for ourselves reveals that we have painfully lost sight of the dreams and visions that once painted our future. These words should bring a halt to the anguish and tears that can be traced to self-pity and doubt. Their words should weaken the foolish thinking that has caused so many of us to divorce ourselves from all humanity, and made too many beggars in a land of abundance. Their thoughts and deeds should put an end to that achy, timid heart replete with pain and disappointment. Their outlook on life should terminate the miserable existence that seeks fear instead of hope; hatred but not love; and greed rather than compassion. Their personal philosophy should stifle the uneventful life that has become little more than a string of endless days of boredom and monotony.

Drawing from a wellspring of knowledge that surpasses all understanding, and powered by a faith that others call unconquerable, these trusty souls leave you and me one final question to ponder: What is the full measure of an individual's life? Is it how *great*? Is it how *much*? Or, is it how *good*? I am confident you will find the answer. Simply put, when it comes to life, these women refuse to lose. And what do they know? Just the basics: love, kindness, patience, faith, prayer, and "that God don't make no junk." In all honesty, I learned more about life and living from just one of their letters than from three years in graduate school. In the days and years to come, I hope their wisdom becomes a steady source of inspiration for you, too.

Blessings,
Dennis P. Kimbro, Ph.D.

Complete List of Grandmothers Whose Letters Are Profiled

Kattie J. Adams
Orlando, FL

Daisy W. Alston
Hampton, VA

Rosalie Andrews
Marietta, GA

Naomi W. Arnold
Lithonia, GA

Georgia Atkins
Washington, DC

Yvonne Atwell
Nova Scotia, Canada

Leola Harrison Banks
Houston, TX

Ferdine Barrett
Baltimore, MD

Thelma Bartholomew
Brooklyn, NY

Mary C. Blackmon
Cleveland, OH

Lezlie R. Bishop
Atlanta, GA

Catherine J. Brent
Yazoo City, MS

Betsy Brown
Wilmington, DE

Mary L. Brown
Newport News, VA

Bessie Adam Burks
Houston, TX

Marie Burnett
Hampton, VA

Harriet Chinn
Columbus, GA

Geraldine B. Clark
Hampton, VA

Ursena N. Coleman
Houston, TX

Gloria Cosgrove-Greene
Oceanside, CA

Jannie Coverdale
Oklahoma City, OK

Lula B. Daniel
Birmingham, AL

Nerva L. Daniel
Gadsden, AL

Yolanda Daniels
Atlanta, GA

Angela Davis
Cincinnati, OH

Frances Diaz
Harlem, NY

Fannie Dickerson
Brooklyn, NY

Willie M. Dismuke
Bernice, LA

Laurie Drummond
Baltimore, MD

Annie Mae Duncan
Farmville, NC

Shirley Eastland
Waco, TX

Gladys Young Flack
Shelbyville, TN

Betty Ford
West Covina, CA

Sadie B. Gandy
Cincinnati, OH

Carrie V. Garrow
Hampton, VA

Doretha Gilliam
Baltimore, MD

Denise Gines
Decatur, GA

Cora R. Goodwin
Nashville, TN

Ella Goolsby
Decatur, GA

Shige Graves
Junction City, KS

Milla Jean Grayson
Bellflower, CA

Ophelia Green
Waipahu, HI

Ruth P. Green
Atlanta, GA

Yvonne D. Greer
Milwaukee, WI

Annie B. Gregory
Hampton, VA

Linda C. Gresham
Chicago, IL

Lenora Grissom
Indianapolis, IN

Darnell Grubbs
Wichita, KS

Annie Gunn
Atlanta, GA

Mae Hamby
Nashville, TN

Natalie J. Harrell
Decatur, GA

Ann Harris
Decatur, GA

Mary Harris
Milwaukee, WI

Estella Kincaid Harvey
Milwaukee, WI

Gladys Hester
Atlanta, GA

Maude Hinton
Hampton, VA

Rosie Hodges
Chicago, IL

Elizabeth "Mother"
Howell
Port Huron, MI

Rosie Howze
Morristown, NJ

Korine Hudson
Hampton, VA

Willie P. Hunt
Atlanta, GA

Bertha Johnson
Birmingham, AL

Emma Jean Johnson
Pearl River, LA

Eva Johnson
Cleveland Heights, OH

Johnnie Mae Johnson
Palmdale, CA

Clara Jones
Charlotte, NC

Elizabeth Jones
Chattanooga, TN

Elder Sharon T. Jones
Washington, DC

Gertrude Jordan
Philadelphia, PA

Myrtle Joyce
Houston, TX

Flora Kelly
Waterloo, IA

Deborah Lestage
Decatur, GA

Christiana Lewis
West Orange, NJ

Emma Lowe
Atlanta, GA

Peggi Mackenzie-Young
Dartmouth, Nova Scotia,
Canada

A. G. Maute
Legon-Accra
Ghana, West Africa

Rosemary Wynne
McCauley
Staunton, VA

Ruby McCauley
Oklahoma City, OK

Gladys McClain
Opalocka, FL

Linda Howard McKinnie
Decatur, GA

Calevea McQuarters
Tulsa, OK

Delories Miley
Dothan, AL

Ethel Moore
New York, NY

Laura Justice Moss
Pittsburgh, PA

Jessie L. Mouton
New Orleans, LA

Mary Murray
Baltimore, MD

Marion E. Nixon
Brooklyn, NY

Diana Onley-Campbell
Washington, DC

Leoney Orie
Hampton, VA

Elizabeth Pitts
Douglasville, GA

Minnie Player
Birmingham, AL

Yvonne Pointer-Triplett
Cleveland, OH

Doris Price, Ph.D.
Glenmora, LA

Addie Pugh
Birmingham, AL

Sarah A. Reed
Atlanta, GA

Jean Rhodes
Decatur, GA

Yvette Ridley
Chicago, IL

Martha Rodgers-James
Hopewell, VA

Jeannie Rogers
Cincinnati, OH

Clara Villa Rosa
Harlem, NY

Jewel B. Ross
Bryan, TX

Gladys Russell
Toledo, OH

Marian Scarborough
Baltimore, MD

Dorothy Scott
Louisville, KY

Zimmie Shelton
Atlanta, GA

Jeri Shipp
Indianapolis, IN

Ila Shoulders
Port Huron, MI

Lucille Singleton
New York, NY

Daphne Sloan
Chattanooga, TN

Bessie Lee Hawkins Smith
Swan Lake, MS

Cansada Smith
Houston, TX

Jane E. Smith, Ed. D
Washington, DC

Myrtice Smith
Atlanta, GA

Bernice Stepney
Hampton, VA

Ellen A. Stewart
Hampton, VA

Sarah Stewart
Hampton, VA

Delores A. Tabb
Odenton, MD

A. J. Taylor
Washington, DC

Vivian E. Thomas
Atlanta, GA

Deborah William
Thompson
Atlanta, GA

Dolly C. Turner
Washington, DC

Millie Turnipseed
Decatur, GA

Enid M. Tyler
Baltimore, MD

Mennie Lou Tyus
Memphis, TN

Lovenia T. Wamget
Atlanta, GA

Eleanor F. Weekes
Newport News, VA

Mildred Whiney
Chicago, IL

Katie P. White
Euclid, OH

Leola Whitlock
Lake Providence, LA

Julie G. Williams
Hampton, VA

Betty Wilson
Baltimore, MD

Mother Mary Ann Wright
Oakland, CA

Dorothy L. York
Indianapolis, IN

Carolyn J. Young
Baltimore, MD

Printed in the United States
by Baker & Taylor Publisher Services